D1558976

Pastor, Staff, and Congregational

Relationships:

Through Servant Leadership and Quality Administration

BERNIE M. SPOONER, PH.D.

Compiler and General Editor

ROSS WEST, D.MIN.

Publishing Consultant and Process Editor

Christian Leadership Publishing
Coppell, Texas

Bernard M. Spooner, Compiler and General Editor
Ross West, Publishing Consultant and Process Editor

ISBN – 13: 9781492131175
ISBN – 10: 1492131172

Subject Heading: Religion / Christian Ministry / Pastoral Resources

This book is dedicated to the pastors, staff, and congregations with whom I have been privileged to serve, and particularly to Dr. James E. Coggin and to Carolyn, his incredible wife and partner in ministry. They, along with the congregation of Travis Avenue Baptist Church, Fort Worth, Texas, nurtured my wife Pat and me, and later our children, as we served and matured with them over a period of thirteen years.

Table of Contents

Introduction

By Bernard M. Spooner, Ph.D... *vii*

About the Writers ix

Part 1. Church Staff and Congregational Relationships

1. The Call of Christ for Believers
    By Howard Batson, Ph.D. *1*

2. Servant Leadership: The Place to Begin
    By C. Gene Wilkes, Ph.D. *21*

3. The Pastor Relating to the Staff
    By Phil Lineberger, D.Min. *39*

4. Developing Good Staff-to-Staff Relationships
    By Norma S. Hedin, Ph.D. *57*

5. Pastor and Staff to Congregation Relationships
    By Randel Everett, D.Min... *73*

6. Developing Good Congregation-to-Staff Relationships
    By Bill Brian, J.D. *87*

7. Christian Ethics in Church Relationships

    Part A: Practicing Christian Ethics in Pastor, Staff, and
    Congregational Relationships
    By Larry C. Ashlock, Ph.D. *109*

    Part B: The Congregation Relating Ethically to the
    Pastor, Staff, and Other Congregations
    By William M. Tillman, Ph.D. *117*

Part 2. Quality Staff Administration Essential

8.   Staff Administration: Foundation for Good Staff
     Relationships
     By Bernard M. Spooner, Ph.D...*127*

9.   Planning with Staff and Congregational Leadership:
     Dynamic Planning Relationships
     By Morlee Maynard, D.Ed.Min. *149*

10. Conflict Resolution in Staff and Congregational
     Relationships
     By Blake Coffee, J.D. *167*

11. Leading a Church When Moral Failure Occurs
     By Larry C. Ashlock, Ph.D. *189*

Appendix I. Job Descriptions
     By Robby Barrett, D.Min. *205*

Appendix II. Notes on Personnel Policies
     By Robby Barrett, D.Min. *225*

Introduction

BY BERNARD M. SPOONER, PH.D.

The Purpose of This Book

This book fills the need for a fresh, comprehensive resource for building quality relationships among pastors, church staff leaders, and members and leaders in churches. Often in this day of fast-paced changes, conflicts arise that might have been avoided if intentional attention had been given to relationships. This book has been written by a team of experienced pastors, staff leaders, and laypeople who have demonstrated effectiveness in building healthy churches.

This volume begins with a sound biblical and theological foundation related to the call to ministry for both vocational ministers and all believers. All Christians are called, but all serve according to their gifts and abilities. The approach of the book is that servant leadership and good personnel administration are essential to quality staff and congregational relationships. Also, this book assumes that the pastor leads the church, and the pastor and vocational staff are called to help equip the congregation for the ministry to the community and beyond.

Because of the current context in churches, a chapter on the congregation relating to the pastor and staff and a chapter on conflict resolution are included in the book. A decision was made to ask active church leaders who are also attorneys to write on these subjects. Furthermore, the book treats the important issues of staff and congregational ethics and addresses the serious problem of moral failure.

Who Needs This Book?

University and seminary professors will find this volume a good choice for a textbook for preparing ministers for church ministry. It will also be a valuable tool for pastors, general staff leaders, and lay leaders in local churches.

Some Possible Uses of This Book

- The book could serve as a textbook for a university or seminary course on *church and church staff relationships.*
- It could also be used in university and seminary courses on *church administration.*
- This volume could also be used as a resource for university and seminary *internship courses for ministry students.*
- Parts of the book could be *studied by staff* in a staff retreat or over a period of time in regular staff meetings.
- Parts of the book could be taught to the *church deacons, church committees, and other church leaders* in a retreat setting or as leaders and committees are oriented for a new year of service.
- *Personnel committees* could be given copies to read as they think through their work, for a full discussion on church staff administration is included in the book.

About the Writers

Larry C. Ashlock, Ph.D.,
executive director, Baptist Center for Global Concerns, Arlington, Texas; fellow and professor of Pastoral Leadership and Ethics and director of Doctor of Ministry Program, B. H. Carroll Institute, Arlington, Texas

Robby Barrett, D.Min.,
minister of education, First Baptist Church, Amarillo, Texas

Howard Batson, Ph.D.,
pastor, First Baptist Church, Amarillo, Texas; former chair of Baylor University Board of Regents

Bill Brian, J.D.,
attorney, Courtney, Countiss, Brian and Bailey, L.L.P., Amarillo, Texas; former member of Baylor University Board of Regents

Blake Coffee, J.D.,
founder and executive director of Christian Unity Ministries, San Antonio, Texas

Randel Everett, D.Min.,
pastor, First Baptist Church, Midland, Texas; former executive director of the Baptist General Convention of Texas

Norma S. Hedin, Ph.D.,
fellow and professor of Foundations of Education, director of Master's Degree Programs, B.H. Carroll Theological Institute, Arlington, Texas; adjunct professor of Research, Gary Cook Graduate School of Leadership, Dallas Baptist University

Phil Lineberger, D.Min.,
pastor, Sugar Land Baptist Church, Sugar Land, Texas; former president of the Baptist General Convention of Texas and frequent curriculum writer for BaptistWay Press®

Morlee Maynard, D.Ed.Min.,
professor of Christian Education; director, Doctor of Education Ministry Program; and director, Christian Education, Midwestern Baptist Theological Seminary, Kansas City, Missouri

Bernard M. Spooner, Ph.D.,
professor and associate dean, Graduate School of Ministry, Dallas Baptist University, Dallas, Texas; former director of Sunday School/Discipleship Division of the Baptist General Convention of Texas

William M. Tillman, Ph.D.,
director of Theological Education, Baptist General Convention of Texas, Dallas, Texas; formerly professor of Christian Ethics, Logsdon School of Theology, Hardin Simmons University, Abilene, Texas

C. Gene Wilkes, Ph.D.,
president, B. H. Carroll Institute, Arlington, Texas, and also fellow and professor of New Testament and Leadership; formerly pastor of Legacy Drive Baptist Church, Plano, Texas

Ross West, D.Min.,
Dallas, Texas, publishing consultant and process editor for this book; formerly publisher of BaptistWay Press® (retired); veteran publishing professional, curriculum planner, and Christian education leader

PART 1:
Church Staff and Congregational Relationships

Chapter 1

THE CALL OF CHRIST FOR BELIEVERS

By Howard Batson, Ph.D.

Just like people, churches have reputations. Some churches are known for being harmonious, mission-minded, and committed to their community. Other churches, however, are perceived as being divisive, self-centered, and estranged from their neighbors. Moreover, a church's reputation involves more than just a collection of positive or pejorative adjectives.

Among pastors and staff members, there is much "table talk" about the reputations of various congregations. Recently, I heard a potential pastoral candidate for a megachurch make this comment: "I'm considering telling the search committee that I am not interested. You and I both know that congregation has been under the iron fist of deacons for decades; their pastors are mere puppets." Other churches, in contrast, find their leadership centered in a "pastoral dictator" who gives little more than lip service to the ideas of congregational governance and committee participation. Still other congregations find their locus of leadership in the church staff. In this paradigm of power distribution, the pastor plays the role of preacher, while executive pastors, staff coordinators, and administrators cast the vision and manage the ministries that meet the daily needs of the congregation. Every congregation operates within one or more of these three systems of leadership. The pastor, the people, or the staff members operate individually or collectively to cast the vision and empower the ministries of each community of faith.

During a recent interview for a staff position, a potential employee inquired, "Who provides the real leadership for First Baptist Church of Amarillo?" His question was a worthy one that I had never carefully considered. Pausing to ponder, I finally replied, "I know that in most churches, the largest part of leadership is provided by the pastor, the laity, or the staff. Our church, however, engages all three spheres of influence in an inclusive approach to leadership." The church has had pastors such as J. Howard Williams, Carl Bates, and Winfred Moore with tremendous vision and a hands-on leadership style. At the same time, each of these pastors encouraged and welcomed the lay leadership to share both in vision casting and decision making. Not to be excluded, the church has engaged talented staff members who exercise a great deal of autonomy within boundaries set by the pastor and lay committees. "I can't define exactly how it works," I explained to the potential staff member, "but all three spheres coexist without squelching or limiting the involvement of the others." It is unclear how this shared leadership approach developed through the years at First Baptist Church, but I am thankful for its existence. Serving together, each of these three elements of leadership generates a greater good than any single category could provide.

In this chapter, I am going to explore a biblical understanding of the call and purpose of each of these three important segments of the leadership triangle in the ministry of the church. As a result, I'll attempt to answer these key questions: *Who is called into ministry? Does a difference exist between the call of a pastor and the call to all disciples? What is the New Testament approach to church leadership? How does the church staff complement both the leadership of the pastor and the congregation?* Balancing the roles of people, pastor, and staff, this chapter will examine a biblical paradigm for each segment of leadership.

Calling All Disciples

Unfortunately, a "them/us" distinction sometimes exists between clergy and laity that is probably the result of both the willingness of the laity to yield their responsibilities to "professionals" and the temptation for ordained ministers to slowly, even if not intentionally, take over the ministry functions of the church.[1] The distinction between clergy and laity, although real, must be carefully understood lest the role of church members be limited by a notion of "professional ministry."[2] In reality, the essence of following Jesus is following a call. Jesus began his ministry in the Synoptic Gospels by declaring that the kingdom of God had arrived. Soon thereafter, he approached a group of fishermen on the Sea of Galilee and called, "Follow Me, and I will make you become fishers of men" (Mark 1:15–17, NASB; see also Matthew 4:17–22).

Unlike the Catholic tradition,[3] the Protestant reformers primarily understood the idea of "calling" as the broadest "call" to Christian discipleship and faithfulness to the Christian community.[4] Indeed, even a cursory reading of the New Testament would prevent us from making too much of the distinction between those who are called to "vocational ministry" and those who volunteer.[5] The Greek word for calling, *kaleo*, and its derivatives are used in a theological sense about seventy times, forty of which are from Paul's writings.[6] Sometimes the word is used to denote the calling of individuals to a specific ministry, such as that of Paul and Barnabas on the "first" missionary journey (Acts 13:2) or of Paul and company to Macedonia (Acts 16:9–10). Most often, however, the word is used for the calling that comes to all who would dare to follow Jesus. For example, there is an inclusive call to salvation. Jesus himself declared, "I did not come to call the righteous, but sinners" (Matthew 9:13, NASB). The primary call on both laity and clergy is the call to find salvation in following Jesus. To those who have chosen to follow him, moreover, Christ issues a call to a life of holiness (Matt. 5–7). Paul, more specifically, declared to the church at Thessalonica, "God did not call us to be impure but to live a holy life" (1 Thessalonians 4:7, NIV84). Paul repeated the idea when he spoke to his son in the faith, Timothy: "God...has saved us and called us to a holy life" (2 Timothy 1:9, NIV84).

Be careful before you answer the call of Christ, however, because it may also encompass an element of suffering. Peter wrote to those suffering under Neroian persecution, "To this you were called, because Christ suffered for you, leaving you an example, that you should follow in his steps" (1 Peter 2:20–21, NIV84). More encouraging, however, is our call to freedom. In Galatians, we read, "You, my brothers, were called to be free. Do not use your freedom to indulge in sinful nature" (Galatians 5:13, NIV84).[7]

Given the passages just cited, the very essence of following Jesus and being part of his people is to answer a call. In fact, *ekklesia*, the Greek word translated as "church," is composed of two other Greek words, *ek* (out of) and *kalein* (to call). Hence, the definition of being part of the church is to be among the "called out ones."[8]

A real tragedy occurs when "paid professionals" begin to take over the basic ministries of the church. Following the apostles' paradigm, the basic function of pastors and teachers is to equip the saints for the work of service to the building up of the body of Christ (Ephesians 4:11–12).[9] The Gospel of Matthew reveals that all Christians are to fulfill the Great Commission (Matt. 28:18–20). By virtue of our being disciples, we are to witness and proclaim the Lordship of Christ Jesus to all who need the presence of his kingdom.

In the megachurch culture, we have witnessed the ministries of "paid professionals" take over the ordinary functions of church members. Churches often find it easier to hire paid staff than to recruit volunteers. As a result, the megachurch menu of professional staffers offers a plethora of personnel, such as these: social justice pastors, community life directors, parking lot ministers, web page associates, spiritual formation pastors, and worship arts ministers. Although no individual position on the list is inappropriate, a danger exists when followers of Jesus try to "pay off" professionals to fulfill their basic call to discipleship and service.[10] *The church can never employ enough staff members to fulfill the duties of all who would dare call Jesus Lord.*

A recent trend, noted in church bulletins and on web pages, shows how superficially sophisticated job titles have become for ministers. Responding to such frivolity, one blogger gives us some suggestions: Instead of pastor, use "Director of Spiritual Journey" or "Architect of Journey-Oriented Life Vision." For the minister of music—no one wants to use that old term anymore—use something like "Experiences Coordinator" or "Sensory Engagement Specialist." For the education minister, we could make a much bigger splash if we use a term like "Spiritual Formation Coordinator." The youth minister—how blah is that? How about the "Molder of Emerging Generations"?[11]

In healthy congregations, staff members are greatly surpassed in energy and effort by dedicated members who have made serving in the community of faith the passion of their lives. While serving on a university board, I noted that institutions of higher education often boast of a small student-to-faculty ratio. Outstanding universities seek to have one professor for every ten to twelve students. Concerning a church's member-to-minister ratio, however, the measure of success is inverted. The more we equip and empower the saints, the more we reflect a New Testament model. *In a truly vibrant congregation, the paid ministers are few, and the people are passionate about the ministries of the church.*

The task of pastors and staff members is to help every church member realize that his or her primary calling in life is to follow Christ and serve his kingdom, even though the member earns his or her living as a plumber, schoolteacher, banker, or physician. All of Jesus' followers have divine appointments to be Jesus' presence as they engage in their vocation, whether they are employed in the ministry or the marketplace. From a New Testament perspective, our "day job" is a means to ministry. In our secular positions, we earn resources to empower our church, and we form relationships that allow us to introduce our coworkers to the Lordship of Jesus. Like the tentmakers (Aquila and Priscilla, Acts 18:1–3), sellers of fabric (Lydia, Acts 16:14–15), and law enforcement personnel of the first century (Philippian jailor, Acts 16:27–33), we are to bear the hope of the arriving kingdom.

God calls people from every vocation to serve his church, even as they stay engaged in secular endeavors. I get most excited when I see school principals, landscapers, and clerical employees passionately devoted to the ministries of the church. They are not paid to serve, but they have found their primary identity in being followers of Jesus and members of his community of faith. Every day, in every encounter, they seek to be the priestly presence of the body of Christ to a broken world. Their priorities are radically different from those of their unbelieving counterparts. Derek Tidball, visiting scholar at Spurgeon's College, concludes:

> Throughout the New Testament there is a noticeable absence of any reference to leaders in the church being "priests." The church has assumed a priestly role, and every member is now a priest, with privilege and direct access to God through Christ the high priest, and has the attendant responsibility to offer "spiritual sacrifices." The longed-for hope of Exodus 19:6 has at last become a reality in the church.[12]

The emphasis on the priestly role of all believers undermines any pretense that paid leaders in the Christian church are somehow in a class of their own.

Leading the Called

Having established that all Christians are called into ministry as part of the call to follow Christ, is there any way individual believers may also be called to a position of leadership, such as that of a pastor or staff member? Paul used the adjective "called" seven out of the ten times it is employed in the New Testament. Two of those seven cases occur in Romans 1. Of particular interest is the fact that Paul employed "called" in two distinct ways in Romans 1. In verse 6, he referred to all believers in the capital city as "called of Jesus Christ" (NASB). The idea of "called" stresses God's initiative. Christians are people whom God has chosen. For Paul, the called are those "of Jesus Christ" (Romans 1:6, NASB), meaning those who belong to Jesus Christ. Put simply, once we are called, our lives are Jesus Christ's. Responsibility comes with every call to follow the Christ.[13]

While Paul certainly referred to all believers in the city of Rome as "called," he also used the same adjective in regard to his position of leadership as an apostle. In Romans 1:1 (NASB), as Paul introduced himself as the sender of the letter, he labeled himself as "a bond-servant of Christ Jesus, called as an apostle." Paul wanted us to know that he was not self-appointed or chosen by people. He was, rather, called by God. For Paul, the idea of "called" carries with it the idea of response. The "called" are those who have not only heard but have also responded to God's divine bidding. As demonstrated in Romans 1, the New Testament supports both the idea that all Christians are "called" by God and the idea that specific Christians are "called" to roles of leadership.

Lest any pride develop within the hearts of those called to ministries of leadership, Robert Dale reminds us that the primary model for biblical leadership is that of servanthood. Did Jesus not say that the one who wishes to be the greatest must be the servant among us (Matt. 20:27–28; 23:11; Mark 9:35; 10:43–44; Luke 9:48; 22:26–27; John 13:14)? The Synoptic Gospels, moreover, contrast the lording of secular rulers with the humility of Christian leaders (Matt. 20:20–28; Mark 10:35–44; Luke 22:24–27).[14]

The Baptist emphasis on the priesthood of all believers creates something of a problem. We have long stressed the ministry of the laity, the position of priest for all believers, and even believer's baptism as something of a commissioning service to ministry for the kingdom.[15] With this elevated view of the laity, Baptists sometimes find themselves unclear about the status and role of both clergy and deacons. In the midst of this tension between church leaders and the inherent ministry of all who profess the Lordship of Christ, we must find a place that does not diminish the priesthood of all believers and yet recognizes the seriousness of "calling out the called" within the community of faith. [16]

As Jesus Christ is our great High Priest, he has interceded once and for all on behalf of the people of God. He now sits enthroned at the Father's right hand. Through this ministry of reconciliation, every believer has been made a priest before God. Therefore, even as the temple's curtain of division is rent in two, each believer now has the authority in Christ to enter into the Father's presence. Baptists have correctly respected the ministry of the laity.

Although they hold functional offices within the community of faith, neither pastors nor deacons have claim to some superior priestly position by virtue of their ordination.[17] In Baptist tradition, ordination is not seen as a sacrament but a symbolic setting apart to a more intense or specialized ministry or missional task within the household of faith.[18] As Alton H. McEachern, a Baptist pastor, has concluded, "Those ordained are 'first among equals' and are honored not for their position, but for their faithfulness as they function and exercise their gifts in ministry."[19] Therefore, as Baptist scholar William L. Lumpkin concluded, there is no essential difference between clergy and laity. Ministers are, in essence, laypeople appointed to special tasks for which they show the evidence of a spiritual gift.[20]

The Baptist position on the priesthood of believers finds its roots in the aftermath of the Reformation. The medieval tendency of ascribing to ordination a sacramental power that made a clear distinction in essence between clergy and laity was rejected by the Protestant reformers. They depicted the laying on of hands as a distinction in function alone. Despite the fact that the priesthood of believers has had no greater enthusiast than Martin Luther, and although he boldly proclaimed the equality of the shoemaker with the bishop, Luther himself concluded that the public ministry of the word "ought to be established by holy ordination as the highest and greatest function of the church."[21] Moving beyond the traditional reformers, radical reformers demonstrated an even lower view of ordination. Yet, even among the radical reformers, the practice of laying on of hands remained as a sign of commissioning for ministerial tasks—preaching, baptizing, and teaching.[22]

Setting Apart for Service

Lest we overemphasize the priesthood of believers to the exclusion of God's selective call, we must remember that biblical tradition is rich with the story of God calling and setting servants apart for kingdom functions. The biblical account depicts a setting apart for special ministry tasks and distinctions of service based on gifts and calling. Throughout Scripture, the concept of God's selectivity is paramount. One can hardly read the stories of the patriarchs without recognizing "a scandal of particularity—God calls particular people for particular tasks and sets them apart to serve."[23] Israel is selected as a particular people, and, even within the particular people, prophets, priests, and kings are selected.

The story of the people of God is the story of God's own selection of individuals to serve him in unique tasks of ministry. Throughout biblical history, for example, God has called men and women to special roles as servants. Samuel was just a young boy when God called him to serve. Although the call came in the quietness of the night, it came with increasing clarity (1 Samuel 3). God called Joshua to lead the nation of Israel into the Promised Land (Joshua 1). Jeremiah pleaded for a release from his burdensome service because the call just seemed too crushing (Jeremiah 20). Amos was called to leave sheepherding to become a spokesman to a wayward nation (Amos 1). Deborah was called as a prophetess, a judge, and a hymnodist to fill a major role in the deliverance of Israel (Judges 4). Hers was a ministry of the word expressed in sermon, song, and counsel.[24]

Jesus himself placed a special call upon the Twelve, the Apostles, to walk in a daily relationship with him, set apart to preach the good news of the gospel. Saul of Tarsus experienced a dramatic call on the road to Damascus, after which he became the apostle to the Gentiles (Acts 9).[25] Aquila and Priscilla, a husband-and-wife team, served as bivocational missionaries and tentmakers (Acts 18). Phoebe was a deaconess (Romans 16), and the four daughters of Philip prophesied (Acts 21).[26] The canonical witness leaves an open door for a called or set-apart ministry. God's method of working among his people has long involved calling, sending, and empowering individuals for special responsibilities.

A call to servant leadership can be understood, therefore, as working in tandem with the priesthood of all believers. While all who call Jesus "Lord" are workers for the kingdom, the community calls out and transfers a unique responsibility (*not* a special status) to some of its members for the purpose of a defined task of ministry.[27] The doctrine of the priesthood of believers need not work in conflict with the concept of ministerial leadership. Both biblically and historically, these two ideas work together for kingdom purposes.

Following Biblical Models

A study of the history (Acts) and letters (Pauline, Petrine, and Johannine epistles) of the New Testament church yields helpful insights into the community's developing leadership structure. A survey of the letters of the New Testament confirms that there were individuals exercising leadership among the congregations (1 Thessalonians 5:12; Rom. 16:1; Colossians 4:17; Philippians 1:1). From the Acts of the Apostles, we learn that leaders were to be "filled with the Holy Spirit" and directed by him (Acts 4:8, NASB; see also 6:3, 5; 7:55). Paul and Barnabas appointed elders in the churches they planted (Acts 14:23; see also 20:18). In the pastoral epistles, we learn that the "elders" were those who "direct the affairs of the church" (1 Timothy 5:17, NIV84; 3:5). Sometimes Paul called the congregational leaders elders (*presbyteroi*); other times he called them overseers (*episkopoi*). These two words, for Paul, were interchangeable. He slipped from using the word "elder" to "overseer" with the greatest of ease (Acts 20:17–18, 28; Titus 1:5–7).[28] The attributes of the elders/overseers found in the New Testament are numerous. They:

1. Administer the offering for benevolent purposes (Acts 11:29–30)

2. Are appointed by Paul and his associates to serve (Acts 14:23; Titus 1:5)

3. Are selected by the Holy Spirit (Acts 20:28)

4. Preside over practical and theological decisions of the church (Acts 15:2, 4, 6, 22, 23; 16:4; 21:18)

5. Are to be on the alert for those who teach false doctrine (Acts 20:31; Titus 1:9–10)

6. Are listed alongside deacons as leaders in the church (Phil. 1:1)

7. Receive honor when they lead well (1 Tim. 5:17)

8. Teach and preach in the churches (1 Tim. 3:2; 5:17)

9. Are to live respectful lives with a resulting good reputation (1 Tim. 3:1–7; Titus 1:7)

10. Should be properly compensated for their labors (1 Tim. 5:18)

11. Are not to be accused of wrongdoing without solid witnesses (1 Tim. 5:19)

12. Are to receive the laying on of hands only after being examined (1 Tim. 5:22, perhaps in reference to ordination)

13. Are to administer pastoral care to the sick (James 5:14)

14. Are to shepherd/pastor the flock of believers with a servant's heart (1 Pet. 5:2–3; Acts 20:28)

15. Are not to be greedy for sordid gain (1 Pet. 5:2; 1 Tim. 3:3)

16. Are to serve with eagerness (1 Pet. 5:2)

17. Are to be conscious of the accountability they will give to the chief shepherd/pastor, Jesus Christ (1 Pet. 5:4).

Considering the plethora of references to leaders in the early church who were called as elders/overseers (pastors), we can conclude with certainty that the apostles saw no contradiction between the call issued to all who follow Christ and to those who were called to positions of leadership. Peter, for example, clearly set forth the priesthood of all believers (1 Pet. 2) but also made reference to the presence of elders who were specifically called to pastor the flock (1 Pet. 5).

Pastors in the Plural

While it is true that Peter saw himself as an elder among the elders (1 Peter 5:1), no biblical model demands that leadership be placed exclusively in the hands of a single pastor. In fact, in the Pastoral Epistles (1 and 2 Timothy, Titus), the word for elder, *presbyteroi*, is always in the plural form. While this could mean that there was one leader in each separate household church, more than likely it implies that each house church actually had several elders. From a New Testament perspective, it is probably best to view the staff that works alongside the pastor as co-elders with their supervisor. To be sure, efficiency and clarity may demand that one elder supervise the others (1 Pet. 5:1).[29] Paul showed no reluctance to serve in a supervisory role to Timothy and Titus, and James was clearly a key leader who exerted great authority over decisions made in the early church. At the same time, however, churches would be healthier if they did not focus so much on the role of a single elder within the congregation. In fact, some churches operate with co-pastors, with more than one individual leader assuming the role of supervising the church staff. Many pastors, moreover, begin their role of leadership in a ministry other than senior pastor.

Both pragmatically and theologically, we cannot make major distinctions between the call of the pastor and the call of staff members who serve alongside the pastor as part of the church's leadership team. Some staff members are not equipped to serve as senior pastors. Paul's letters, however, indicate that various people are gifted by the Spirit with various spiritual gifts to lead the congregation. Some are prophets; some are teachers; some minister to the sick; and some are administrators (see 1 Corinthians 12:8–10, 28).[30]

However we might see the role of the minister in the New Testament, the reality is that each minister, whatever his or her spiritual gifts, is to be focused on letting the gospel of Jesus Christ

Deacons

Deacons serve as an interesting hybrid between laypersons and staff members. The origin of deacons is often traced back to the appointment of seven in Acts 6. The apostles wanted to devote themselves "to prayer and to serving the word" (Acts 6:3, NRSV). Therefore, others were selected to serve the daily needs of the congregation. The word "deacon" carries the implication of helper or servant. In Philippians 1:1, we have a reference to both "overseers" and "deacons." In 1 Timothy 3, we are given similar but separate qualifications for the offices of overseer and deacon.

Whereas overseers (pastors) are to exercise the gift of teaching, no mention is made of a deacon's ability to teach. In most churches, deacons assist the pastor and staff (the overseers or elders) in carrying out daily ministry to the congregation. No church can possibly employ enough ministers to care for every need of the congregation.

At First Baptist Church of Amarillo, a deacon makes a daily visit to members of our church family who are in a hospital or rehabilitation facility. Our church family is organized into smaller "flocks" that are each assigned to the care of a deacon. A strong deacon ministry is a sign of a healthy church.

have its full impact in people's lives. Pushing against plays of power, Derek Tidball concludes, "A model that is hierarchical, authoritarian, abusive, singular, exalts personality, or any model that exalts tasks to the exclusion of relationships, or growth to the exclusion of truth, would not be legitimate."[31]

The expectations many people have of their pastors are both unrealistic and certain to lead to disappointment and failure.[32] Pastors are expected to be pals with the children, excellent biblical exegetes, financial gurus, program organizers, volunteer recruiters, moral guides, denominational figureheads, ecumenical advocates, social activists, and gospel evangelists, not to mention a media personality ready to conduct an interview with the local television station at a moment's notice. Pastors must learn to share some of these tasks with their fellow elders, staff members who are gifted in these special areas of ministry. While all ministers must, at times, do tasks beyond their expertise and comfort level, dividing the care for the congregation is a healthy New Testament model.

Calling Through a Community

Fred Craddock, Bandy Professor of Preaching and New Testament, emeritus, at Candler School of Theology, remembered going to summer camp at Bethany Hills every year as a teen. He had fond memories of summer camp: playing, eating, making friends, and having fun. Frank Drowota, the pastor of the Woodmont Christian Church in Nashville, Tennessee, was a minister at the camp. Craddock said he would never forget the evening when, as the campers left the dining hall, Drowota walked along with him and asked, "Can I talk to you?"

"What'd I do wrong?" Craddock responded.

The pastor said, "Have you ever considered becoming a minister?"

"No, sir, never, never have." Craddock was seventeen years of age and about to begin his senior year in high school. He recalled that Drowota "ruined everything for me." Craddock continues,

> What a thing to lay on a kid. All I wanted to do was go where the girls were, save some money to get a car, go to school some more, someday get married, have a house, a garden, and two weeks of vacation in the summer....And then he lays that on me. I thought about it when I got up in the morning; I thought about it when I went to bed at night. I'm still thinking about it. He was a minister, and he did that.[33]

Craddock's story highlights the point that the call to ministry should not be a personal one alone. The call to ministry is, in every sense, a community event. The historic example of George W. Truett's call illustrates the community's role. As Truett was growing up, he was repeatedly urged to become a minister. But he was adamant in his determination to be a lawyer. One Saturday in 1890, Truett attended a covenant meeting. He recalls:

> When they got through with the rest of the church con-ference...the oldest deacon...rose up and began to talk.... "There is such a thing as a church duty when the whole church must act. There is such a thing as an individual duty when the individual must face duty for himself. But it is my deep conviction as it is yours—that we have talk-ed much one with another—that this church has a duty to perform and that we have waited late and long to get about it. I move, therefore, this church call a presbytery to ordain Brother George W. Truett to fulfill the work of the Gospel ministry."[34]

Truett protested, imploring them to desist, but the church refused to hear his pleas. That Saturday, the motion carried, the presbytery was summoned, and Truett was ordained. Reflecting on the community's responsibility to call her leaders, William H. Willimon says, "All talk of clergy which neglects the ecclesial origin of the pastoral ministry is dangerous."[35] Willimon argued that the "inner call" is more associated, historically, with the monastic life than the life of community leadership.

There is a tendency among seminary students to avoid service in a local church. The students want to be professionals, ministers, and servants of the kingdom of God, but they look to parachurch organizations and social service entities, avoiding a direct relation-ship with the local church at all costs. They want to experience ministry apart from a relationship with and accountability to the local church. The truly incarnational approach to ministry, becoming one with church members, seems much too demanding and dangerous. These students have heard the horror stories from the church field, and so they try to steer clear of the local bride of Christ. This self-appointed, as opposed to church-appointed, approach to ministry is foreign to biblical foundations and the historic traditions of Baptists.

My own call to ministry is better described as a community urge than an individual urge. The community called Leawood Baptist Church in Greenville, South Carolina, urged me to consider entering the gospel ministry, from middle school onward. The community selection process was slow but sure, until finally, without any official notice, it was assumed by all around me that I would become the pastor of a local church. Affirmation after preaching on youth Sunday, a word of encouragement after teaching an adult Bible study class, and the recognition of my keen interest in studying Scripture all combined to guide that community to direct me into ministry.

As Willimon wrote, "We are called to leadership in the community of Jesus Christ through the community."[36] Both Calvin and Wesley spoke of the "two-fold call," composed of an inner call that is confirmed by the outer call from the community.[37] Those called to community leadership must never forget the one or two people who believed in their call early on and, in a sense, really ordained them.

Conclusion

Half a century ago, the best and the brightest among our students were encouraged to attend seminary and enter the ministry. Some have feared that there is currently a "brain drain" among the new leaders of the church. Historian Jim Singleton expressed the situation in stark terms. Around 1950, 10 percent of all Phi Beta

Kappa college graduates became ordained clergy; today it is less than one-tenth of 1 percent.[38] Perhaps this paucity of the gifted among the called has to do with the church's failure to encourage students, under the leadership of the Spirit, to enter the ministry.

In 1960, a young man who might be trying to decide between medical school, law school, or seminary would quickly be encouraged to give his very best to God by giving consideration to ministry in a local church. Today, however, when young men or women mention they are considering "church work," family members, friends, and even practicing ministers offer discouraging words: "Oh, you'd better be sure. The hours are long; the pay is low; and the members are unrealistic in their expectations."

The church needs to stop apologizing for selecting its gifted (intellectually, socially, or artistically) and move forward, under God's leadership, to call men and women into the ministry—calling them from among the called.

Review Questions

1. In what distinct ways is "call" used in the New Testament?

2. Are there any distinctions between an elder and an overseer?

3. How do contemporary staff positions compare to leadership roles in New Testament churches?

4. How does the Baptist concept of the priesthood of the believer contribute to or conflict with the idea of being "called into ministry"?

5. What role does the church play in the call of individuals into places of leadership?

Suggestions for Further Reading

Howard K. Batson. *Common-Sense Church Growth.* Macon, GA: Smyth & Helwys, 1999.

Alice R. Cullinan. *Sorting It Out: Discerning God's Call to Ministry.* Valley Forge, PA: Judson Press, 1999.

Eugene Peterson and Marva Dawn. *The Unnecessary Pastor: Rediscovering the Call.* Grand Rapids, MI: Eerdmans, 2000.

Derek Tidball. *Ministry by the Book: New Testament Patterns for Pastoral Leadership.* Downers Grove, IL: InterVarsity Press, 2008.

Chapter 2

SERVANT LEADERSHIP: THE PLACE TO BEGIN

By C. Gene Wilkes, Ph.D.

God's call on your life is the beginning of your leadership. Call gives birth to leadership because call gives you a purpose or reason to lead. When God called Moses to lead the people of Israel out of Egypt, Moses became a leader—albeit a reluctant one—and he then had a clear mission and destination for his leadership. This chapter will help you to lead where God has called and planted you to serve.

Servant Leadership: The Best Way to Lead

Servant leadership—designed after the model and teachings of Jesus—is the best way to accomplish the shared mission and vision of the church. The essential nature of leadership is *influence*. An accepted definition of leadership is "...a process whereby an individual influences a group of individuals to achieve a common goal."[39] This process of influence moves people from the status quo toward a new reality envisioned by the leader. Jim Collins applied what he learned from *Good to Great* businesses to the social sector and concluded, "True leadership only exists if people follow when they have the freedom not to."[40] Leading in a freely gathered group of people around a cause or purpose like the church is a challenge.

What does biblical leadership look like? Don N. Howell, Jr., concludes that *biblical leadership* "...is taking the initiative to influence people to grow in holiness and to passionately promote the extension of God's kingdom in the world."[41] Or, more simply put, Henry and Richard Blackaby describe *spiritual leadership* as "...moving people on to God's agenda."[42] Combining both the secular and biblical descriptions, we can say the biblical or spiritual leader uses his or her natural, positional, or God-given influence to motivate others to achieve a common goal: God's mission and vision.

Servant leadership is also about influence, but in this model, influence finds its source and direction in God's call to become directly involved where God is working in the world in order to accomplish God's purposes. Servant leadership as defined in this chapter meshes well with the leadership descriptions already mentioned and the model of our Leader, Jesus. Following Jesus' example and teaching, a servant leader leverages his influence to "...serve the mission, and lead by serving those on mission with him."[43] This definition highlights the leader's focus on God's call/mission on his life and his efforts to serve others to accomplish that mission. For example, the Apostle Paul described himself as a "servant [to the church] by the commission God gave me" (Colossians 1:25, NIV). He also saw himself as "a servant of [the] gospel by the gift of God's grace given me through the working of his power" (Ephesians 3:7, NIV). God called Paul to expand the message of Jesus to the ends of the earth, and Paul accepted that assignment as a servant to the one who sent him.

As the pastor or staff member, you will have influence from the position the church gives you. The essential issue, then, is for whom and for what purpose(s) will you exercise that influence? A biblical model of leadership calls for the mission of God to be the focus for your leadership and for those who follow you. The servant leader called by God uses his or her influence to call and equip others to accomplish God's plan.

Servant Leadership Is Needed in All Fields of Work, Especially in Church Leadership

Servant leadership is needed in every arena of leadership. Why? Servant leadership falls in the broader category of transformational leadership, which is "a process that changes and transforms people" and "...involves an exceptional form of influence that moves followers to accomplish more than what is usually expected of them."[44] Rather than influencing others through transactions such as promised promotions and benefits earned through increased or improved performance, servant leaders seek to transform people through two key behaviors: they put followers first, and they support the followers' personal development.[45] This emphasis on the priority and development of the followers leads to exceptional performance, achieved goals, and increased morality of both the leader and the followers.

Servant leadership is especially needed in leading the church, which is composed of the people Christ empowered with the Holy Spirit and released on a mission to make disciples of every ethnic group (Matthew 28:19–20). Jesus not only exemplified many of the characteristics identified by secular observers[46] but also modeled leadership submitted to the Father's mission for his life (John 6:38) and served those he called to join him on that mission. Ultimately, Jesus laid down his life for those he came to rescue (John 15:13; Mark 10:45). Jesus' focus was to complete the Father's mission first and then to train his followers to do the mission he commissioned them to complete. He transformed lives through a personal, ongoing relationship with them.

This model to carry out the mission of God and to train others to complete that mission with us identifies the core practice of a servant leader in the local church. What are some principles or guidelines surrounding these core practices?

Some Leadership Principles or Guidelines

The Mission Is Everything

Mission answers the question, "Why are we here?" or "Why are we doing this?" Ask people in your church why your church exists, and you may get as many answers as the number of people you ask. Without a clearly stated purpose or mission, you are left to cater to the personal preferences of those you lead. As followers of Jesus, we begin with the first mission Christ called his disciples to complete: "As you go, make disciples of all ethnic groups" (Matthew 28:19, my translation). Does your church gather and scatter to make disciples—to transform those far from God into those willing to die for Christ?

Mission is everything for the servant leader. When Jesus came to Peter to wash his feet, Peter resisted Jesus' act of service toward him. Jesus told his chosen leader among the disciples, "Unless I wash you, you have no part with me" (John 13:8, NIV). Peter had his own ideas about who Jesus was as the Messiah and why the group had been formed. Jesus, leading dressed like a servant and acting like a slave, did not allow Peter's personal perspective to stand. All this—even Jesus' service to wash Peter's feet—was to complete the Father's mission call on Jesus' life to be the suffering servant Messiah. Peter understood and told Jesus, "Not just my feet but my hands and my head as well!" (John 13:9, NIV). Jesus did not allow the personal preferences of his follower to change the course of his mission to be the suffering servant Messiah.

Mission is the leader's benchmark for making decisions. If your church's mission is "to make disciples of all ethnic groups," you have a way to evaluate ideas and programs with regard to their effectiveness to complete the mission. For example, if someone comes to you and says that, for the last five years, the church has held an all-church garage sale in the church parking lot to raise money for school supplies, you would ask, "How does this help us make disciples?" If there's a direct correlation between the garage sale and what your church describes as a disciple, go for it. If not, direct your efforts and funds to something that does correlate. This same mission alignment is true for a third-grade Sunday School class. Does what you do on Sunday morning with third graders contribute to making age-appropriate disciples of Jesus?

Ask these questions to detect whether the mission is everything for those you lead:

- Are you able to write or say, in one sentence, God's mission call on your life and for those you lead?
- Can those you lead articulate *why they do what they do?*
- Is your mission the benchmark for decisions, or is it just a statement on a poster somewhere?
- Does the shared mission of the group drive the planning and efforts of the group?

Servant Leaders Have a Clear Picture of Where They Are Going
Vision is the leader's compass. Vision answers the question, "Where are we going?" It is the leader's true north for the group he or she leads. Without a clear description or picture of the future, followers will create their own and lead others to it, or they will wander around like lost sheep, looking for the next patch of green grass, which is always greener than where they are. Servant leaders passionately call others to God's future for their lives.

Vision answers the question, "Where are we going?"

A popular description of vision is "an ideal and unique image of the future."[47] That time-honored definition matches Jesus' example of calling people to follow him into a new future for their lives. Jesus challenged people, "Repent, for the kingdom of heaven has come near" (Matt. 4:17, NIV). People were to get their hearts right with God and change how they lived because Jesus had brought the kingdom of heaven near to them through his presence.

How did they know what the kingdom of heaven looked like? Jesus told stories or parables about the kingdom. They generally began with a statement like this: "The kingdom of heaven [or God] is like...," and Jesus would then tell a story of a lost coin, a waiting father, a mustard seed, or a pearl of great value. Each story described some aspect of where Jesus was leading them. Servant leaders have stories from their lives to describe what God's future looks like. These may be in the form of life change for those who are becoming disciples of Jesus or of examples of ministries that model what you want others to become.

Mission drives, vision draws. Vision inspires and creates passion. Bill Hybels, pastor of Willow Creek Community Church, describes vision as "a picture of the future that produces passion."[48] Servant leaders lead by painting God's picture for the future for those they lead. This is not necessarily a vision from God flashed in a lightning bolt; it can be a mosaic patched together by a group of leaders committed to seeking the heart of God for his people. Either way, the picture must be clear and compelling for those they lead.

Ask these questions about vision for the group you lead:

- Can you describe to those you lead where you are leading them?
- Does what you describe inspire passion in them?

- What is a story or two from real life that describes what you are leading people toward?
- Do the people you lead have a shared vision for the future, or are they working to create a number of future realities?

Servant Leaders Equip Others to Lead

To equip someone answers the question, "How do I do this?" "This" is the mission or the person's assigned task or goal related to the mission. If people are clear on why they are doing what they do and know where they are going, they want to know how to do their part to make the vision a reality. You can't invite a group of people to climb Mount Rainier in Washington and not train them to reach the summit and climb back down safely. Servant leaders serve those they lead by equipping them to realize the shared vision.

The Scriptures teach us that Christ gave the church "...some as apostles, some as prophets, some as evangelists, and some as pastors and teachers, to equip the saints for the work of ministry, that is, to build up the body of Christ" (Eph. 4:11, 12, New English Translation). The biblical word for *equip* comes from the ancient contexts of fishing and medicine. In both arenas *equip* means to prepare for an activity, like making nets for the next cast or setting a bone to heal. What would it look like if you saw yourself as one who equipped or prepared people "for the work of ministry" rather than teaching them the latest curriculum? From this vantage point, you teach people skills for living as a follower of Jesus rather than simply giving them more information for their workbooks.

Equipping others is discipleship.

Jesus used the "follow me" method of discipleship. Everything Jesus did and said was a lesson in skills to live as kingdom people.

From teaching the Sermon on the Mount (Matt. 5—7) to casting out demons who knew his true identity (Mark 1:33–34), Jesus modeled and taught what a changed life living in his kingdom looked like. He was more like a coach on a sports team who taught and honed skills for the game than a teacher who passed out outlines of a subject to the students and then left the room.

Ken Blanchard and Phil Hodges equate a servant leader to that of a performance coach. They claim, "Coaching is the most important servant leadership element in helping people to accomplish their goals."[49] Some you lead are novices who require detailed instruction and guidelines. Others are like apprentices who need your direct attention. Still others grow to work independently, and some become highly skilled and able to coach others.[50] As a servant to those you lead, you adjust your leadership skills to match their needs in order to reach shared goals.

One reason leaders burn out is that they try to do all the work themselves. They have bought into the myth of the Lone Ranger leader who rides into town, defeats evil, and rides off into the sunset a hero. J. Oswald Sanders says, "There is no virtue in doing more than our fair share of the work."[51]

Doing most of the work on your own says more about your ego than your ability to lead.

Servant leaders share their responsibility and authority to meet the needs and goals of the church. To assign a responsibility without authority demotivates. Responsibility *with* authority frees one to excel.

These questions will help you assess your ability to equip others:

- When was the last time you delegated a significant task to someone? How much work are you taking home at night?
- Are you more like a teacher or a coach? What are the levels of development of those you lead?
- Have you trained people with the skills they need to complete the job or task you have delegated to them?
- Have you delegated the right amount of authority to achieve the responsibility you have given a person or a group?

Servant Leaders Build Teams to Meet a Need or Reach a Goal

A team of leaders built around the mission and vision answers this question for those you serve and lead: "Whom can we count on?" If there is only one leader who knows the mission, vision, and how to carry it out, and that leader is taken out, to whom will they turn and on whom can they rely to take them to the next level of growth? This is one reason churches suffer organizational whiplash every two years on average when a new pastor joins them. There is no team of leaders aligned with the mission and vision and who share leadership with those they lead. So, each leader guides the church in his or her perceived direction until it's time to go to the next church. After a history of this pattern, churches tend to resist any change brought by a new pastor or staff member.

Jesus built a team of leaders into which he invested his life 24/7 for three or more years and then commissioned them to continue in what he had come to do: make more disciples of all people. He was the only one, true Son of God, and only he could complete the mission the Father sent him to finish. After Jesus ascended into heaven, however, the Twelve became the leaders of the kingdom movement called the church. Empowered by the Holy Spirit, they turned the world upside down with the message of Jesus and lives that reflected their Leader's suffering, sacrificial love.

Whatever you call the subgroups to which the church gives responsibility and authority to meet a need or reach a goal—committees or teams—they are essential to accomplishing your mission. Bill George, former CEO of Medtronic, remembers, "As a leader, I have always surrounded myself with people who are more knowledgeable and experienced [than] I am. The key is having people around you who complement your weaknesses and make up for your lack of experience."[52] Too often, pastors and staff members seek to compensate for their weaknesses and lack of experience with more effort and inauthentic behavior rather than trust others enough to team with them.

Blanchard, Hybels, and Hodges observe, "Effective leaders working at the team level realize that to be good stewards of the energy and efforts of those committed to work with them, they must honor the power of diversity and acknowledge the power of teamwork."[53] A team of leaders is more powerful than a single leader.

A team of leaders is more powerful than a single leader.

Ask these questions to test your team-building focus:

- Do those you lead know the team they can count on to take them where they are going?
- Write the names of people you trust and with whom you are sharing leadership.
- Who offsets your weaknesses? Who makes up for your lack of experience?
- If you left your place of leadership, who would carry on the mission to which you have given yourself?

Some Pitfalls to Avoid in Leadership

Avoid the Trap of Management Instead of Leadership

Too often the pastor and staff are expected merely to take care of who shows up and to keep existing programs running. If you do this, you may see yourself more like a store manager than the leader of a movement. Sometimes a congregation evaluates staff on their effectiveness in keeping the number of complaints down rather than in producing changed lives. Many times the pastor and staff find their days choked with recruiting volunteers and attending committee meetings that have to do with maintenance of the institution and nothing to do with the mission. Yet, God's call burns in their hearts to follow Jesus into the mission field to reach the lost and to make disciples who make disciples.

The proven adage penned by Warren Bennis, "The manager does things right. The leader does the right things,"[54] is true for pastors and staff in a local church. Doing things "right" or as they have always been done can become the priority of one's time and talents. However, doing the "right thing" is God's desire for those who serve the people of God. Yes, you must manage resources (both people and materials), plans, and the execution of plans. But those efforts at managing must serve the greater goal of making progress toward meeting a need or reaching a goal related to the mission.

Max DePree says, "The measure of leadership is not the quality of the head, but the tone of the body. The signs of outstanding leadership appear primarily among the followers."[55] You manage things. You lead people. Don't make the mistake of trying to make yourself look good by managing things. Invest in those who follow.

To avoid the trap of management, ask these questions:

- When I am done with this meeting, what tangible things have we done to change people's lives?
- Am I sitting on a committee or playing on a team?
- Is this more about preserving the past or creating the future?
- If we quit doing this, would anyone outside the program miss it?

Avoid Letting Setbacks and Conflict Discourage You

Leadership creates conflict. Ask Moses, Deborah, Jesus, or Paul. Servant leadership—influencing others to join God on mission— requires challenging the status quo and creating a new future. Abraham had to leave the comfort of Ur to experience the blessings of God. Peter and Andrew had to leave the familiar life of a fishing business to follow Jesus to establish the kingdom of God.

Leaders experience opposition from those they lead because the leaders challenge their followers' current situation in order to help them experience God's future for their lives. Heifetz and Linsky see leadership as bringing adaptive change to a group in order to meet needs for which the group does not have easy answers. They observe, "People rarely elect or hire anyone to disturb their jobs or their lives." This is one reason they conclude that "leadership requires disturbing people—but at a rate they can absorb."[56]

This "disturbing people" in order to meet needs and experience God's vision for them will bring conflict and pain in a leader's life. Paul, the apostle to the Gentiles, boasted in the scars of conflict he felt as he brought the good news of Jesus to Jews and Gentiles alike. He cataloged his trials and suffering in a letter to the Corinthians, but he concluded, "If I must boast, I will boast of the things that show my weakness" (2 Corinthians 11:30, NIV. See his entire list in verses 16–33.) J. Oswald Sanders wisely observes, "Scars are the marks of faithful discipleship and true spiritual leadership."[57] Every biblical servant leader called by God to establish his will and ways on earth faced opposition and conflict.

Setbacks do not have to discourage you. They can be exercises that strengthen you. You can learn valuable leadership lessons from conflict. J. Robert Clinton observes:

> The things learned can include: the nature of conflict, ways to resolve or avoid conflict, ways to use conflict creatively, how to identify conflict with God's processing, and how to see conflict as the stimulus for other processing. The emphasis should be not just on the insights learned about conflict, but also on the intended development [of the leader] orchestrated by God in those conflict situations.[58]

Setbacks do not have to discourage you. They can be exercises that strengthen you.

Conflict can both expose and develop the character of a leader. Conflict can be God's crucible of character development and spiritual growth.

Ask yourself these questions to help you through a time of conflict:

- What setbacks have discouraged you?
- What have you learned from conflicts in your ministry?
- Have you asked God to help you "boast in your weaknesses"?
- How has God developed your character through times of conflict?

Avoid Evaluating Yourself and Your Ministry by the Culture's Metrics of Success

Pastors and church staff members are tempted to measure the success of their work by using cultural norms of growth and success. One of the unwritten norms in our culture is "Bigger is blessed," and we tend to compare our work with that of ministries that are bigger than ours. Sometimes this results in our feeling guilt and shame. Other unwritten points of comparison are what I call the four Bs: Baptisms, Budgets, Buildings, and Bodies. If those counts are larger on the attendance chart each year, then all is well. If not, the leader (and many members) begins to worry about the health of the group. However, it is not the nature of the body of Christ to grow earnings and sales volume like businesses. The church is more like a "body" (1 Cor. 12:12–14), and Paul reminded the Corinthian Christians they were "God's field, God's building" (1 Cor. 3:9, NIV). Nurturing a body, growing crops in a field, and constructing a building have measures of success beyond "more is better."

Neil Cole writes, "As I read the New Testament, I have found three things that Jesus views as crucial to the success of his followers. They are faithfulness, fruitfulness, and finishing well."[59] Rather than finishing with the largest church or in the most visible position among your peers, God calls servant leaders to find their success in being faithful to his call on their lives, producing fruit in the lives of others, and finishing well when they exit a mission field—or life.

Here are some questions to evaluate your success before God:

- How do you currently measure success? Do those you lead know these measurements?
- Have you been faithful to God's call on your life? to your spouse? to your family? to your church?
- Does your life produce the fruit of the Holy Spirit's presence in your life? (Galatians 5:22–23)
- Have you helped produce fruit in the lives of others? (John 15:8)

- Do you have a plan of succession and exit that will benefit the church more than it benefits you?

Avoid Using Power and Authority for Personal Gain

Power and authority are the currency of leadership. Your position alone will give you these assets to lead people into God's new future for them. The danger, however, is that you could use those assets for your personal gain or advantage. When Jesus held an impromptu leadership seminar on the side of the road, he reminded his disciples that to "lord it over" or "exercise authority over" others were recognized ways of influencing people toward a goal. The Romans were experts at lording it over Israel in Jesus' day, and the religious leaders adeptly exercised their religious authority over the people of Israel. Jesus turned the use of power and authority on its ear when he told his students, "Not so with you" (Mark 10:43, NIV). In Jesus' kingdom, leaders were to act differently.

Jesus described a great leader as someone who would be willing to use the assets of leadership as a servant and to become a slave to the group if needed. Jesus set the standard for the use of power and authority among God's people when he proclaimed, "For even the Son of Man did not come to be served, but to serve, and to lay down his life as a ransom for many" (Mark 10:45, NIV84). Jesus used his power and authority as "the Christ, the Son of the Living God" (Matt. 16:16, NIV) to serve others at their greatest point of need: a right relationship with Holy God. We who lead like Jesus will follow Jesus' example to meet the spiritual, physical, and emotional needs of others.

Jesus described a great leader as someone who would be willing to use the assets of leadership as a servant and to become a slave to the group if needed.

Check your use of power and authority by answering these questions:

- In what ways do you have the opportunity to use your power and authority to lead others?
- How does your use of these leadership assets match Jesus' example and teaching about them?
- Where have you been tempted to practice leadership for your personal gain or advantage?
- In what ways do you exercise "not so with you" leadership like Jesus?

Prayer and the Life of a Servant Leader

J. Oswald Sanders says, "In nothing should the leader be ahead of his followers more than in the realm of prayer. And yet the most advanced Christian is conscious of the possibility of endless development of his prayer life."[60]

Prayer is to the leader what communication is to a marriage. With authentic, care-filled communication, a marriage can thrive for a lifetime. Without it, even a covenant made before God will falter and fail. Why do servant leaders believe they can lead without constant communication/prayer with their Leader?

Prayer is the servant leader's lifeline to God. Jesus was in constant contact with the Father who sent him. Luke describes Jesus' daily habit and extended times of prayer (see, for example, Luke 5:16; 6:12; 9:28; 11:1). John's Gospel tells us that Jesus did not speak unless the Father spoke first (John 12:49–50) and that Jesus led with a sense of timing because he knew the heart of the Father (compare John 2:4 with John 17:1). Jesus was honest enough in prayer to ask whether there was another way to complete his mission, but he humbled himself and prayed, "not my will, but yours be done" (Luke 22:42, NIV). The servant leader Moses had an intimate prayer relationship with *Yahweh*. We are told, "The Lord would speak to Moses face to face, as one speaks to a friend" (Exodus 33:11, NIV). Paul wrote to his friends to "pray continually" (1 Thessalonians 5:17, NIV) and to gear up for spiritual battles that would be part of their experience as Christ's followers (Eph. 6:10–18). Prayer is essential to the effectiveness of God's called servant leaders.

Servant leaders are honest with God. They pray what is on their hearts and speak boldly before the Lord. David cried out, "Do not abandon me, O Lord. Do not stand at a distance, my God" (Psalm 38:21, New Living Translation). Richard Kriegbaum, former president of Fresno Pacific University, wrote a prayer for use when the leader considers introducing a change. You may be able to relate when he prays:

> Is this change even possible? I need to feel sure I have not missed a fatal indicator. There is a fine line between faith and folly. Maybe we can't leap this far; two leaps won't work across a gap. Protect me from leading us off the edge. Confirm that we can make it.[61]

Leaders who call others to change their lives in order to join God where God is working have prayed a form of this prayer before.

Servant leaders pray for those they lead and serve. I am convinced "that no servant leader should stand to lead until he kneels to pray with those he serves."[62] Robert Clinton concurs: "If God calls you to a ministry, then he calls you to pray for that ministry."[63] The unique character of Christian leadership is the privilege to pray for and with those you serve and lead. It is not only the source of strength and guidance from your Leader, but it is also the wellspring of compassion and insight into the lives of those you lead.

Review Questions

1. Read a definition for servant leadership, and write your own definition.

2. What is the role of "mission" in servant leadership? What is your one-sentence mission statement?

3. Describe the difference between "mission" and "vision."

4. Briefly discuss "burnout" in ministry. What does this say to the leader?

5. Briefly discuss the statement, "A team of leaders is more powerful than a single leader."

6. List the four pitfalls to avoid in leadership.

Suggestions for Further Reading

Along with the books referenced in the endnotes for this chapter, consider these resources:

Ruth Haley Barton. *Strengthening the Soul of Your Leadership: Seeking God in the Crucible of Ministry*. Downers Grove, IL: IVP Books, 2008.

Ken Blanchard, Bill Hybels, and Phil Hodges. *Leadership by the Book: Tools to Transform Your Workplace*. New York: William Morrow and Co., 1999.

James C. Hunter. *The Servant: A Simple Story about the True Essence of Leadership*. Roseville, CA: Prima Publishing, 1998.

Alan J. Roxburgh and Fred Romanuk. *The Missional Leader: Equipping Your Church to Reach a Changing World*. San Francisco: Jossey-Bass, 2006.

Chapter 3

⤺

THE PASTOR RELATING TO THE STAFF

By Phil Lineberger, D.Min.

The pastor of a local church has the opportunity and responsibility of leading a team to fulfill the vision and ministry of that local church. How effectively the pastor leads this team will determine for the most part how well the church accomplishes her vision and ministry. To lead the staff team effectively and productively, the pastor must give attention and guidance to a number of critical elements. All of these critical elements involve pastor-staff relationships. The goal of this chapter is to point out some guidelines that will help develop and maintain good pastor-staff relationships.

Needed for Positive Staff Relationships

Staff Relationships Thrive On Clear and Reasonable Expectations

First Corinthians 14:8–9 states, "Again, if the trumpet does not sound a clear call, who will get ready for battle? So it is with you. Unless you speak intelligible words with your tongue, how will anyone know what you are saying? You will just be speaking into the air" (NIV84).

For the purposes of this chapter, consider that speaking "intelligible words with your tongue" means *communicating clearly the expectations for each staff member*. The pastor, as staff leader, plays the central role in communicating clearly those expectations. The pastor's role as *chief communicator* enables staff members to be more effective in their calling and responsibilities. It is crucial that the pastor communicate the vision of the church and the expectations of staff members in supporting that vision.

How will staff members know how to get ready for the spiritual and practical battles of church ministry if there is no clear call from the leader of the staff? How will the staff know how to work together to accomplish the task before them? How does your work support the mission of the church?

A Staff Member Needs to Understand How His or Her Work Supports the Mission of the Church

Management expert Peter Drucker suggests asking five essential questions to determine whether one's work supports the mission of the organization. First, what is our mission? Second, who is our customer? Third, what does the customer value? Fourth, what are the results? And fifth, what is our plan?[64]

George Cladis puts it this way: "The first step in building a collaborative team is to ensure that the purpose of the team is clearly defined and generates enthusiasm. There should be a sense that the team's purpose is God given and God directed."[65]

Understanding that the team's purpose is God-given and God-directed begins with a clear and understandable job description. This job description will seek to answer at least five questions for the staff member: Why am I here? What is my job? Who is my supervisor? How will my job be evaluated? Where are the resources I will need?

In his best-selling book on corporate effectiveness, *Good to Great* author Jim Collins writes, "If we get the right people on the bus, the right people in the right seats, and the wrong people off the bus, then we'll figure out how to take it to someplace great."[66]

A clear and understandable job description is essential for getting the right person on the bus in the right seat. When the right person is on the bus in the right seat, the task of maximizing the gifts of that person becomes more effective. Job descriptions are essential.

As the *Church Staff Handbook* by Harold Westing states,

> Job descriptions spell out duties, responsibilities, and limits of authority in a particular position. Even though every possible situation cannot be written out showing where authority needs to be displayed, some guidelines must be provided for doing so....More staff conflict arises here perhaps than any other place. To whom and under what circumstances is a person to be accountable is one of the major ingredients to be clarified.[67]

Each job description should be in writing. It should be reviewed personally and slowly with the relevant staff member with opportunities for questions and clarifications. It should be included in an employee handbook that also lists the job descriptions of other staff positions.

A job description should include not only the essential requirements of the position but also the manner in which the requirements

What Should Be Included in a Job Description?

1. <u>Biographical data</u> (written for a person already on staff, not for a job opening). This would include job title, person's name, date, and when the job description should be updated.

2. <u>Ministry purpose.</u> When a person is engaged in this ministry, he or she will seek to accomplish the goals listed.

3. <u>Ministry responsibilities.</u> Here, list the various segments of the ministry or program.

4. <u>Working relationships.</u> This will identify the one to whom and for whom the person is accountable.

5. <u>Opportunities.</u> Include extracurricular activities such as seminars, conventions, and other ongoing educational experiences.

6. <u>Qualifications</u> (to be included for recruiting purposes). This list will include academic, spiritual, and ministry skills, and personality or temperament traits.

are addressed. Every pastor leader has certain personal expectations for staff. They could include what Peter Lowe has called the "Three Qualities of Great Employees": smart, hardworking, loyal.[68] Whatever personal expectations the pastor has of staff members, the pastor should make them clear from the beginning.

Expectations might include the following: The staff member's attire should be clean and neat. The staff member should be on time and prepared for his or her task. The staff member should have a positive and constructive attitude. The staff member should understand the scriptural mandate for work: "Whatever you do, work at it with all your heart, as working for the Lord, not for men, since you know that you will receive an inheritance from the

Lord as a reward. It is the Lord Christ you are serving" (Colossians 3:23–24, NIV84).

A Staff Member Should Understand How His or Her Job Relates to Other Staff Jobs

Work should follow a person's gifts, and these gifts should be used collaboratively. Knowing the job descriptions of the other staff members will help each understand responsibilities and expectations of others. Each staff member needs to know how other staff members contribute to the overall goals of church ministry

7. Financial arrangements. Show first the salary benefits, which would include insurance and vacation time. Second, include business expenses, such as car and entertainment fees. A new job description should also include moving and settlement allowances.

8. The organizational chart. Include in a job description a pictorial representation of the groupings of work, people, and superior/subordinate relationships for all those involved in the organization. To understand his or her role in relation to team members' roles, each person also needs to see everyone's relationship to the boards, committees, and groups.[69]

and to work with other staff members as a team, each accomplishing the tasks assigned to him or her.

As Wayne Cordeiro states, "A full symphony under the direction of a master conductor will always sound infinitely better than a one-man band. As we discover and develop our individual gifts and learn to stroke in rhythm as a team, we will be astonished at how much further and faster we go—and with far fewer injuries!"[70] A staff member needs to know how each member contributes to the overall goals of church ministry and then be given the autonomy to carry out his or her part of the plan.

The staff member also needs to know what he or she can expect of the pastor, such as "accepting and encouraging differing ideas and opinions, never embarrassing a staff person in a team meeting or public arena, having well-planned agendas exhibiting forethought and afterthought, committing to pray, encourage, and provide available resources for the success of both individual team members and the team as a whole, and practicing open, honest, and godly communication."[71] The pastor must set the example for other staff members.

A Staff Member Should Be Aware of How and How Often He or She Will Be Evaluated

Very few people enjoy being evaluated for fear of facing certain truths about their work. We know that no one is perfect, but we dread having our imperfections pointed out in a professional arena. Evaluations are necessary, however, for effective and long-lasting ministry.

We can't improve if we don't know where we need improvement. Management guru Peter Drucker writes, "Now, most of us, even those of us with modest endowments, will have to learn to manage ourselves. We will have to learn to develop ourselves. We will have to place ourselves where we can make the greatest contribution....The only way to discover your strengths is through feedback analysis."[72]

What should these evaluations be like?

(a) Evaluations can be done annually or semiannually according to the nature of the job. However, semiannual evaluations provide the opportunity to reward or correct work before too much time passes.

(b) Evaluations can be done by the supervisor, by the person being supervised, or by one's peers.

(c) Evaluations can be broad-based, listing achievements, goals, and needs for improvement personally and professionally, and they can include action steps.

(d) Evaluations can also be more detailed by seeking answers to direct questions such as these: What have you learned or experienced in the past year that has significantly changed or enhanced your ministry? How would you describe your ideal job? How well do your personal goals mesh with the church's organizational goals? What do you see yourself doing in ministry three to five years from now? What do I want my supervisor to know regarding such things as my overall portfolio of ministry, my job fulfillment and satisfaction, my compensation level, my sense of inclusion as an important part of the team, and my relationship with my supervisor?

Fagerstrom suggests these questions to help with evaluation[73]:

(1) What do I like most about my job?

(2) What do I find most difficult in my job?

(3) Where would I like to learn more and grow?

(4) What one thing would I like to change in my job description?

(5) What would I like to accomplish in ministry over the next year?

(6) What personal goals would I like to consider?

(7) Where do you think I can best improve my performance?

(8) What could I have done differently this past year?

(9) Are there any blind spots I may be missing or avoiding?

(10) How can we serve each other better this year?

(e) Evaluations can be structured in a number of ways—the simpler the better. For instance, the evaluation could be structured around these three criteria: *Exceptional*—In what areas and how has this employee exceeded job requirements? *Good*—In what areas and how has this employee met job requirements? *Needs Improvement*—In what areas and how does this employee need to improve in meeting job requirements?

A Staff Member Should Understand the Rewards and Consequences of His or Her Evaluation

Mediocrity should not be tolerated in a church staff member. To make certain the staff member understands this, there should be rewards and consequences of the evaluation.

The staff member should be rewarded appropriately for his or her performance in those areas of the job that meet or exceed expectations. The rewards should be consistent for all staff members.

The consequences of not meeting expectations should be consistent and fair also. Consequences are not necessarily punishments but rather are wakeup calls for improvement. The consequences should be pointed out by the pastor with positive and concrete suggestions for improvement.

The Pastor Being Attentive to Staff Relationships

Lead in Team Building

Consider what Jesus did in Mark 1:16–18: "As Jesus walked beside the Sea of Galilee, he saw Simon and his brother Andrew casting a net into the lake, for they were fishermen. 'Come, follow me,' Jesus said, 'and I will make you fishers of men.' At once they left their nets and followed him" (NIV84).

In order to build an effective team of disciples, Jesus asked them to come and spend time with him. He intended to give them the attention necessary to build a strong team.

Harold Westing writes, "The strongest form of a relationship works within a framework of honesty, intimacy, and interdependency. A very unhealthy one is characterized by despair, depression, isolation, active addiction, and numbed feelings."[74] By working closely with the Twelve, Jesus built a strong relationship within the framework of honesty, intimacy, and interdependency.

Building a strong staff team requires the same type of attention from the pastor. It requires being aware of each staff member's job, being available to talk about the staff member's ministry, and inquiring about his or her continuing education. The pastor is not only the leader of the staff but also the enabler of the staff. By paying attention to the work of each staff member, the pastor can better enable the staff member to become more effective.

LaFasto and Larson write,

> The kind of energy we associate most often with effective teams, and the kind of energy we find most difficult to understand and explain is spiritual energy. What most people think of as "team spirit" directly influences the amount of productive effort a team will expend: its persistence in the face of obstacles; the willingness of team members to set aside personal egos and cooperate with each other; the capacity of its members to challenge one another and accept suggestions and feedback; how hard it will try to find and correct "problems"; and a great many other important but elusive properties implied by the notion of "spirit."[75]

Be Aware on a Regular Basis of the Work Being Done by the Staff Member

There is a cliché that says, "Don't expect what you don't inspect." The person who leads a staff team needs to be aware of the work being done by each staff member. Being aware requires spending time observing a staff member's work and asking pertinent questions. The pastor should not have to guess what a staff member is doing, and neither should the staff member need to be guessing at what the pastor expects. Open, honest communication on a regular basis provides the light necessary to understand what is being done well and where improvement is needed.

Accountability is necessary to maintain focus on one's job. Accountability is simply paying attention and honoring the work being done.

One formal way to establish accountability (see also the section "A Staff Member Should Be Aware of How and How Often He or She Will Be Evaluated") comes from C. Philip Alexander, a management and organization development consultant.[76] He has offered a simple format for one-on-one quarterly meetings led by the pastor with the staff member. He suggests taking three sheets of paper and dividing each sheet into two sections by a vertical line.

> On the first sheet the staff member responds to the question, "What is your job and what support do you expect of this church and of the senior minister?" On the left hand side of the sheet the staff member states his or her understanding of "my responsibilities to this congregation." On the right hand side the staff person explains "What I need from this congregation and from the senior minister in order to fulfill my responsibilities." This might include such things as more money for postage or secretarial help, the use of a particular meeting room, an hour every week with the senior minister, or additional resources for leadership development.

> The second sheet of paper deals with achievements and needs for improvement. On the left-hand side the staff

member lists his or her achievements during the past quarter. The senior minister may want to add to this list during their joint interview. On the other half of the sheet the staff member lists the needs for improvement covering both personal and institutional deficiencies....

The pastor can add to this list but should keep the emphasis on achievements.

On the third sheet of paper, the staff member lists on the left-hand side his or her goals for the next three months. Then, on the right-hand side, the staff member lists specific steps needed for accomplishing these goals, such as a timeline, resources needed, and how the work on the goal will be evaluated.

Be Accessible to Staff Members

Some pastors cloister themselves away in their office or study and are almost never available to visit with staff members about their jobs or personal needs. This approach leaves staff with the unspoken declaration that the pastor is simply not available to them.

The pastor should let staff members know when he or she is available to visit about their work. A staff member should never be made to feel as though he or she is imposing on the pastor by requesting time to discuss the job. The pastor should come out from behind the desk and sit with the staff member for conversation.

There is no substitute for face-to-face conversation. Face-to-face conversation is the best way to overcome any communication gaps that may be evident. E-mails and phone calls can never take the place of one-on-one personal interaction. Jesus set an example of face-to-face personal contact with his disciples. For instance, we read in Mark 3:13-15, "Jesus went up on a mountainside and called to him those he wanted, and they came to him. He appointed twelve—designating them apostles—that they might be with him and that he might send them

Six Useful Leadership
Competencies[77]

1. Focus on the goal

2. Ensure a collaborative climate

3. Build confidence

4. Demonstrate sufficient technical know-how

5. Set priorities

6. Manage performance

out to preach and to have authority to drive out demons" (NIV84). Again we read in Mark 9:2, "After six days Jesus took Peter, James and John with him and led them up a high mountain, where they were all alone. There he was transfigured before them" (NIV84). Note that Jesus took time to be with them.

Encourage the Staff Member's Growth in His or Her Job

The pastor should encourage staff members to read good books related to multiple areas of ministry, including their own. The pastor might inquire periodically about what a staff member is reading or studying. It is often helpful for the entire staff to be reading a book together and discussing insights from it together in staff meeting.

Encourage staff members to network with other church staff members to learn what they are doing. Provide resources and time for staff members to attend conferences that will provide educational opportunities and personal refreshment.

Handle Potential Problems with Mutual Respect and Support

Note that even Jesus' disciples had conflicts. In Mark 9:33–34

"Conflicts between people often fall into at least four different categories: Perceived conflicts. Potential conflicts. Real conflicts which can be resolved. Real conflicts which cannot be resolved."[79]

we read, "They came to Capernaum. When he was in the house, he asked them, 'What were you arguing about on the road?' But they kept quiet

Ten Don'ts When Conflict Occurs

1. Don't run to another staff person or other ministry leader.

2. Don't run to the senior pastor.

3. Don't create alliances to protect yourself. (Align only with God in prayer.)

4. Don't assume everything is true, affixing blame and making unfair assumptions.

5. Don't let negative perceptions fester and foster an unrealistic scenario.

6. Don't focus on *who* is telling the truth but rather on what *is* the truth.

7. Don't consider revenge or punitive plans.

8. Don't treat a conflict with a cavalier or lighthearted approach.

9. Don't believe that compromise is always a weak or lesser position.

10. Don't offer quick solutions or ultimatums, even if you believe them to be the best. (In a conflict situation, people need time to process and work through a variety of feelings, thoughts, histories, and personalities.)[80]

because on the way they had argued about who was the greatest" (NIV84).

Fagerstrom comments, "Each member has a unique background, spiritual gifts, experiences, longevity, and style—and desires to be recognized for his or her unique contribution.... Where diversity exists, conflict is inevitable. It is the leader's role to bring conflict resolution skills to the table."[78]

Unresolved conflicts have a tendency to go underground and poison the spirit of the team. Conflicts that are allowed to take root can destroy the entire ministry of the church.

Addressing at least three questions can help solve most staff problems:

1. *What is the presenting problem?* To

clarify the presenting problem, explore these questions with the person or persons involved: *Can I put in writing what I perceive as the problem? Is there an initiating circumstance? What is the timeline? What have I done so far to address the problem?*

2. *What is the problem from your viewpoint?* Every problem has various points of view. Each staff member involved in the conflict likely sees it from a personal perspective.

Facts are essential to getting to a responsible approach to problem solving. However, feelings are also very important. What feelings have been generated by a problem? Is there a feeling that someone has not been treated fairly? Emotions must be dealt with as the facts are catalogued. Staff members need to be reminded that they are on the same team and that their actions affect the emotional life of other staff members. Different personalities respond emotionally in different ways to some of the same circumstances.

Finally, the people involved in the problem must be clearly identified. Borrowing someone else's trouble doesn't help clarify and solve a problem. Getting people together who are integrally involved with the problem helps move the problem to a healthy solution.

3. *How can we work out the problem with as little pain as possible?* Be certain that you understand the problem as completely as possible. Through it all, seek God's guidance through prayer and Scripture. Maintain an open mind and spirit to positive conflict resolution. Speak confidentially with those involved in the conflict. Refrain from rehearsing the problem with other staff members not involved in the conflict. Communicate honestly and cordially with those involved in the conflict. List and depersonalize all the options for solving the problem. Come to a consensus and move on.

Express Respect to All Staff, Including Ministry Assistants and Support Staff

Note the strong advice David's military commander, Joab, gave David when David was so focused on himself and his own needs that he neglected those who followed and depended on him: "Now go out and encourage your men. I swear by the Lord that if you don't go out, not a man will be left with you by nightfall. This will be worse for you than all the calamities that have come upon you from your youth till now" (2 Samuel 19:7, NIV84).

Respect and encouragement can help build a healthy culture among staff. If a staff feeds on fear and criticism, the culture of that staff will degenerate into backbiting, cynicism, and despair. The pastor as leader of the staff is most responsible for determining the culture of the staff.

William James (1842–1910) has been called *the father of American psychology*. James is quoted as stating that the "deepest principle in human nature is the craving to be appreciated."

Appreciation multiplies our influence as leaders. What are some things a pastor can do to express respect and appreciation to all staff members?

One thing is to provide open verbal encouragement. When staff members feel valued and appreciated, they are willing to give the extra effort necessary to accomplish their personal and ministry goals. A pastor encouraging a staff member is telling that staff member that he or she is important to the pastor and to the ministry of the church.

Use several different methods to communicate with staff members. Talk with them one-on-one. Give them a call on the phone. E-mail them periodically. Send a text. There are many positive ways to communicate. However, none is better than one-on-one verbal conversation.

The pastor should look for creative ways to compliment and encourage staff members. "Do not withhold good from those who deserve it when it is in your power to act" (Proverbs 3:27, NIV84).

One great way to encourage staff members is to recognize anniversaries and other milestones. Recognizing important events such as work anniversaries, birthdays, and children's accomplishments with something tangible enhances a sense of belonging and value in the staff member. A gift certificate to a nice restaurant for the staff member and spouse, a letter of appreciation, or extra pay with time off creates a climate of respect and appreciation among staff members.

Extend Compassionate Ministry to the Staff Member and His or Her Family

Jesus' compassion can be seen clearly in so many places in the Gospels, such as in John 11:33–35, which states, "When Jesus saw her weeping, and the Jews who had come along with her also weeping, he was deeply moved in spirit and troubled. 'Where have you laid him?' he asked. 'Come and see, Lord,' they replied. Jesus wept. Then some of the Jews said, 'See how he loved him!'" (NIV84). Jesus provides the example for us.

Every staff member is different in skills, emotions, and personality. Each deals with life in different ways. Even so, every staff member goes through predictable phases of growth and development in life. Life is not the same for young newlyweds as it is for parents of teenagers or for adult children of aging parents. Whatever is going on in the life of the staff member comes to the job with the staff member and affects his or her emotions, energy, and outlook.

Pastors need to be close enough to staff members to know about personal needs within their lives and the lives of their families. The pastor also needs to be aware of the resources available to help each staff member get through difficult times.

Maintaining staff members' emotional and spiritual health is crucial to prevent burnout. The pastor needs to lead the church to provide funds necessary to help staff members take care of themselves spiritually, emotionally, and physically. Every staff member needs to be encouraged to take time away for vacation and for training.

We are too civilized these days to believe in human sacrifices—except when it comes to staff members and their families. The family was created before the church, and family members should never be sacrificed on the altar of church ministry. The pastor should be the leader in making family a priority in practical ways. Encouraging days off, family vacations, family traditions, and other family-friendly activities should be a pastoral initiative. Family is a gift of God that needs to be protected, nourished, and celebrated.

Making family a priority is essential to healthy, effective personal ministry.

Review Questions

1. How does a pastor communicate clear, reasonable expectations to the staff?

2. What are some of the essentials to be included in a job description?

3. What practices can a pastor incorporate in paying attention to team building?

4. What are three key questions to be addressed in problem solving?

5. What can a pastor do to express respect to staff members?

6. How can a pastor demonstrate compassion toward his staff?

Suggestions for Further Reading

George Cladis. *Leading the Team-Based Church*. San Francisco: Jossey-Bass, 1999.

Jim Collins. *Good to Great*. New York: HarperBusiness, 2001.

Wayne Cordeiro. *Doing Church as a Team*. Ventura, CA: Regal, 2004.

Peter F. Drucker. *Managing Oneself*. Boston, MA: Harvard Business Review Classics, 2008.

Douglas L. Fagerstrom. *The Ministry Staff Member*. Grand Rapids, MI: Zondervan, 2006.

Carl E. Larson and Frank M. J. LaFasto. *TeamWork, What Must Go Right/What Can Go Wrong.* New York: Sage Publications, 1989.

Carl E. Larson and Frank M.J. LaFasto. *When Teams Work Best.* New York: Sage Publications, 2001.

Lyle E. Schaller. *The Multiple Staff and the Larger Church.* Nashville, TN: Abingdon Press, 1980.

Harold J. Westing. *Church Staff Handbook: How to Build an Effective Ministry Team.* Grand Rapids, MI: Kregel Publications, 2012.

Chapter 4

⌘

DEVELOPING GOOD STAFF-TO-STAFF RELATIONSHIPS

By Norma S. Hedin, Ph.D.

How to Thrive in Associate Staff Ministry, published by The Alban Institute, contains the results of a qualitative study of church staff members. Of the eight results of the study, one of the major findings was that to *thrive* (not just survive) in associate staff ministry, one must have "the ability to develop good working relationships with supervisor and fellow associate staff."[81] This logical assumption, embraced by many who serve as ministers, was aptly documented by the book's author, Kevin Lawson, who conducted twenty-one focus group interviews, and later surveyed more than 400 participants from fourteen denominations in the United States and Canada.[82] The summarized outcome from the study was as follows:

Long-term associate staff members report that support-ive work relationships with their supervisor (normally the senior pastor) and with other associates on staff (if any) are among the keys to thriving in ministry. Healthy and supportive staff relationships can make ministry seem like heaven, even when ministry demands and stresses are high. But relationships with a supervisor or fellow associates that deteriorate into isolation, animos-ity, or indifference can take much of the joy out of even the best of ministry results.[83]

Note that the respondents to the study were *long-term* staff members—defined as those who had remained in staff ministry at least seven years. Since most staff members desire to *thrive* instead of just *survive* in ministry, these findings are significant for ministers and for churches.

"Healthy and supportive staff relationships can make ministry seem like heaven, even when ministry demands and stresses are high. But relationships with a supervisor or fellow associates that deterio-rate into isolation, animosity, or indifference can take much of the joy out of even the best of ministry results."[84]

Not only is the ability to relate to others important if one is to thrive as a staff member, it is also an indicator of character. Don Cousins, former associate pastor at Willow Creek Community Church and currently a leadership coach to Christian leaders, has stated that two indicators reveal character: "how people manage their personal life and how they relate to others."[85] Following a discussion on "leading oneself," Cousins describes the second indicator of character as interpersonal skills:

> Some people can relate only in a hierarchy: up and down a chain of authority. They can work *for* people or *over* people, but they can't work *with* people. If the essence of leadership is to get close enough to people to equip them for ministry, then a key ingredient for success is the ability to work *with* people

> Interpersonal skills involve humility, courtesy, patience, self-control. Someone who exhibits these qualities likely has a healthy character and is eligible for leadership responsibility. Conversely, if a person can't relate warmly to others, I question his or her readiness to lead.[86]

Cousins goes on to say that "relational fit" is important for any team, and so choosing members who fit relationally to the rest of the team makes ministry more enjoyable and also enhances enthusiasm and productivity.[87] So, if positive interpersonal relationships are so critical, what are some suggestions for encouraging these staff-to-staff relationships?

Cultivate a Positive Relationship with Your Supervisor

While positive relationships with other staff members are critical, perhaps the most significant working relationship is between the supervisor (normally the pastor) and the associate staff member. A previous chapter focuses on developing good pastor-to-staff relationships (chapter 3), and so the point here is that it is also important for associate staff members to cultivate a positive relationship with the pastor. One of the primary attitudes is to recognize that the pastor is the leader of the church. Although some pastors focus on more of a team ministry, someone ultimately has to take responsibility for leading the team. To varying degrees, most churches and pastors expect the pastor to take this responsibility. Bruce Powers, in the classic *Church Administration Handbook*, writes clearly on this matter: "The pastor is acknowledged as having the church-assigned responsibility of being first among equals."[88] There are exceptions when the size of the church allows for an executive pastor who would be responsible for the task of leading the staff, but generally the pastor fills this role.

Whether a pastor leads the way a staff member thinks he should lead, respect for the pastor's role as leader, as well as the pastor's decisions and leadership, are necessary. In his article, "The Pastor as Leader of the Staff," Wayne Dehoney provides several analogies that are helpful in thinking about how ministers relate to each other. One is that of a *star*, in which all ministers are parts of one total ministry, "but each staff member is a distinct and equal point of the star in significance and identity as a person."[89] Each is expected to be more proficient in his or her specialized function than any other, but the points are joined together in unity around the total ministry to the whole church. This analogy speaks to the importance of each ministry and the expectations of proficiency in the area of ministry. Another helpful—and common—analogy is that of a *team*. However, he emphasizes the "loyalty and commitment of every staff member to give supreme effort on every play called by the quarterback in the drive toward a commonly agreed upon, predetermined goal."[90] This analogy speaks to the importance of each staff member exerting maximum effort in carrying out the ministry goals of his or her own ministry as well as those of the church.

Note, however, in this latter analogy that the "quarterback" is the one who calls the plays. This illustrates the importance of an acknowledged leader. Dehoney's other two analogies focus on the role of this leader and include the analogy of a *ship* with a captain, the pastor who has been designated by the call of the congregation and who determines the direction of the ship. These decisions include "determining priorities for emphasis, time, monetary and leadership resources."[91] The second one is the analogy of a *van* or vehicle, carrying all of the staff members. While all have input about direction, the senior minister, as the driver of the van, bears the responsibility for getting them to the final destination.[92]

These analogies are helpful to illustrate that all staff members work together and have separate responsibilities and gifts in the church. However, the pastor, as the designated staff leader, must be recognized and respected as the leader of the staff and as leader of the church.

Loyalty to the pastor, loyalty to each other, and loyalty to the church and to the Lord who is served are imperative.[93] Hardee recommends the formation of a covenant to clarify relationships, which would include the "perceptions each minister has about how he or she is to work with every other person on the staff; and clarify how in their working together quality of relationship between and among staff members can be significantly strengthened."[94] Whether a formal covenant or a conversation where relationships are clarified, this recognition of the pastor's leadership is paramount.

Treat All Staff Members as Fellow Believers in Christ

In a landmark study, LaFasto and Larson[95] conducted research with more than 600 teams and 6,000 team members and identified eight characteristics that help teams work best. One of the eight characteristics was *good constructive team relationships*. In particular, this meant that effective teams were able to give and receive feedback well without defensiveness, counterattack, or withdrawal. The ability to be open and supportive of each other and to recognize each person's contribution to the team was essential to effective teamwork.

There are actually two perspectives from which to focus on relationships with other staff members. One of those is related to our theology and the other to practical skills in relating to others. In "A Theology for Healthy Church Staff Relations," William Tuck proposes that the "attitude toward and treatment of one's fellow staff workers are indications of one's theology," since "the practice of ministry is intrinsically involved in one's understanding of theological truth."[96] After a helpful discussion on the role of reconciliation in guiding relationships, based on 2 Corinthians 5, Tuck states:

> Persons who have experienced the forgiving grace of God for their own sins have now become "new creations"—new persons in Christ. Having experienced personal reconciliation, their ministry is to guide others to a similar experience of reconciliation. As agents of reconciliation, they seek now to see people, understand them, and respond to them, not from their old natures, a pre-Christian perspective, but from the viewpoint of those who seek to see, hear, and respond with the spirit of Christ, "for the love of Christ controls us" (v. 14). The guide for relating to others is not simply one's own feelings or desires, but the presence of Christ. "And he died for all, that those who live might live no longer for themselves, but for him who for their sake died and was raised" (v. 15).[97]

This theological perspective reminds us that God's act of reconciliation provided our present relationship to God, and this act overcame our own state of separation, which keeps us from having superior attitudes toward others. Tuck goes on to say that in our awareness of our own "Jekyll-Hyde," character, we should "understand better and be able to be more compassionate toward fellow staff workers when these do things with which they may not agree or approve."[98] He pointedly states:

> It is so easy to judge another's actions and assume that one's own behavior is always superior. But the very willingness to judge so quickly denotes our own state of separation from our fellowman or woman. How easily ministers can forget their own sinfulness and need of forgiveness. Like our co-workers, we, too, stand in the need of forgiveness and should not overestimate our own goodness and minimize others' actions. We both stand on the common ground of God's grace as fellow strugglers in need of forgiveness.[99]

Considering our relationships with other staff members through this perspective of reconciliation helps us to remember that we are modeling biblical teaching and relationships as we serve in our ministries. Other theological perspectives related to this issue might be our view of the church. Paul's image of "the body of Christ" (1 Corinthians 12; Ephesians 2; 4) emphasizes Christ as the "head" of his body the church, with believers as members of it. The descriptions of the church "depict the unity and solidarity of the church, but also the diversity of its members (Romans 12:4–5)."[100] Tuck further makes the point that "No matter what position one has on a church staff, the basic reason for the Church's existence must be kept before us. To lose sight of the Church's mission of continuing the work of reconciliation is to ignore its reason for existing."[101]

Once appropriate theological perspectives are considered, one must also turn to the practical skills of showing forgiveness, care, concern, and interest in fellow staff members.

Practice Relationship Skills

Getting along with others includes demonstrating skills and attitudes that can be learned and practiced. Leonard Wedel, in *Church Staff Administration: Practical Approaches*, states:

> Human relations is people. Working effectively and productively with people is a skill that can be learned. Human relations is knowing how to handle difficult people problems; understanding the motivations of other people as well as your own; and building sound working relationships with many kinds of people....A human relations climate is not built upon a mass approach. It is built upon a person-to-person relationship. It is an individual matter. Each worker senses your personal warmth and concern, your depth of commitment of fair play by the way you consistently respond to him as a person.

> You do not build good human relations in a day or week or month. It's the long haul of days upon days of relationship consistency that ultimately forms your human relations climate.... In fact, building good human relationships may not be so much learning how to get along with others as taking the kinks out of yourself so that others can get along with you.[102]

Although Wedel's suggestions are focused on supervisors, the practical tips he provides are applicable for working with other staff members. He suggests that showing genuine interest in workers, communicating clearly, being courteous (please and thank you), criticizing in private, giving credit where credit is due, fulfilling promises, and admitting one's mistakes are all practical ways to get along with others.[103] Some of the questions he provides to help people evaluate how well they get along with others are listed here:

How well do you get along with others?[104]

1. Are you generally cheerful?

2. Do you manage to keep calm under pressure?

3. Do you keep the promises you make?

4. Do you tend to be impatient?

5. Do you violate personal confidences?

6. Do you give credit where credit is due?

7. Do you make an effort to be a good listener?

8. Do you ignore complaints that appear insignificant to you?

9. Can you refuse a person's request without ill will toward that person?

10. Do you ever ask for opinions or suggestions?

11. Do you make sarcastic remarks?

12. Do you speak in a loud, commanding voice?

13. Do you have a positive attitude?

14. Do you make snap judgments in sizing people up?

15. Are you a moody person?

16. Do you admit your own mistakes?

17. Do you always say "please" and "thank you"?

18. Are you skillful in giving explanations and information?

19. Do you argue?

20. Do you keep postponing requests?

Show Appreciation and Support for Other Team Members

Staff members can be close friends—and often are the closest friends. But even if staff members are not particularly close, it is important for the church that each staff member appreciate and support other team members. It is inevitable that criticism will arise. Criticism should be handled according to biblical guidelines, and team members should be confident that others on the team will be supportive and anticipate the best from each member. Listening to and engaging in gossip is unbiblical, and staff members who engage in such behavior do so at the expense of the team and the ministry. "It is imperative that the members of staff support one another before the congregation. One member of the staff should in no way undermine another; if there are areas of disagreement, they should be taken care of in the staff meeting and not outside in the congregation."[105]

These types of disagreements often occur when staff members collaborate or join ministries together, such as mission trips or church-planting events. Individual staff members have strengths and weaknesses and often criticize other staff members for not doing things the way they themselves would choose to do them. Relationships are strengthened when staff members appreciate the strengths of others. When weaknesses affect a ministry, ministers are to go to each other to discuss their concerns rather than complaining to others in the congregation. While the pastor may be the one who negotiates these relationships, staff members should have the spiritual maturity to handle difficulties in biblical ways.

One of the frustrations of working with other staff members is seeing that one member of the staff seems to be ineffective. Although the inclination may be to let the ineffective staff member experience the results of failure, the reality is that no one wins when a staff member fails in his or her ministry assignment. So one of the commitments to other staff members should be not only the best work that one can do but also a commitment to help other staff members as needed.

Some leaders encourage times of fellowship and recreation together to improve the communication, relationships, and morale of the staff members. Spending a few days together each year in planning, fellowship, and fun can help build positive relationships and appreciation for one another. Playing together as staff members or as families is helpful as well. One suggestion is to just get out and walk around the facility together or play a game in the student facility together. Part of relationships is having fun together, and taking time to have lunch together as a staff, play a round of golf together, or play Ping-Pong together provides an opportunity to laugh together. One leader suggests getting a quartet together to sing in church. (This obviously depends on the skills of the people involved!)

These types of activities are important in building togetherness. Wendell L. Boertje states:

When we are together and familiar with one another we know how to handle the communication signals we send and receive. We can better balance the outgoing and incoming messages in much the same way as the impedance process works in electronics. If we are separated too long we begin to suspect others—what they are saying, doing, thinking, or achieving which might give them advantage over us....One cannot be closed to staff members if he or she is close to them![106]

Closely related to this idea of engaging in activities together—and more important—is taking time to share spiritual life together. Praying in an unhurried way for personal needs, family, ministries, effectiveness, attitudes, and the church in general can make a significant difference in relationships. In an article titled "The Minister of Music in Church Staff Relations," Wendell Boertje suggests that to properly care for other staff members, one must "be interested in their tasks, and support them in their roles," as well as "be close together in time and space. We must budget enough time together for satisfying worship, prayer, planning, sharing, and playing."[107] He suggests the particular role of the minister of music in enriching deeper spiritual life together:

The "God-called" quality brings to a staff a deeper and more sincere commitment and dedication. Expression of this will be found in the contribution of the minister of music to the spiritual life of the staff as it prays, studies, and shares together. The musician becomes a source of spiritual strength and energy, not just a recipient. In addition to an understanding of scripture and theology, the music minister can bring the rich resources of hymnody and music literature to the devotional life of the staff. He or she will be a strong proponent of music and texts which contribute to spiritual growth and understanding.

Such sharing must begin with staff colleagues as together they grow as Christian servants.[108]

This suggestion is true not only for the minister of music but also for all staff members who bring their own spiritual gifts and ministry resources to the deeper spiritual life of staff relationships.

Joe McKeever, an expert responding to questions on BuildingChurchLeaders.com, suggests that part of building healthy working relationships with other staff members includes communicating appreciation for each other publicly.[109] Honoring and showing appreciation publicly not only lets the staff member know that someone appreciates him or her, but it also lets *others* know that one values the ministry and the minister. "Bragging on each other" occasionally is a valuable relationship-building tool.

Focus on Cooperation, Not Competition

One of the byproducts of the individualism in American culture is that we have the tendency to create "silos" for ministry. Occasionally a staff member will describe his or her ministry area as "my ministry." Although this is inevitable to some extent, as part of a team, each staff member should be knowledgeable of all staff ministries. Showing interest in what God is doing in ministries other than one's own can help one appreciate what God is doing in the entire church body, and it can also be a practical help to families in the congregation. In building positive staff-to-staff relationships, showing interest in each other's areas shows support and concern and allows one to pray more specifically for one another and for God's favor on others' ministries.

Positive relationships and support for one another's ministries do require communication. Experts on leadership warn about the tendency for staff members to "get on a little island of their own" and, as a result, fail to connect with other staff members and with the overall mission of the church. Staff members must take advantage of staff meetings, as well as informal conversations, to communicate goals, dreams, plans, and concerns. Some staff members do not speak up during meetings and then feel upset when their views are not considered. As a leader in an area of ministry, it is part of the job to speak up, ask questions, and express concerns in a positive and constructive way. If you have difficulty speaking up or "interrupting," you might communicate this to the pastor and ask for help in involving you in the discussions.

W. L. Howse warned in 1959 that "sometimes staff members make the mistake of planning and projecting a program which is independent of the other work of the church."[110] Although churches today may have a different view on independent ministries, his point is that recognizing that other ministries share the resources of the congregation is critical. With the growth of individualism in American culture, this struggle is ever present. The biblical values of thinking of others more highly than of oneself and being a servant of others are difficult for those of us ingrained with selfishness and self-seeking attitudes. A genuine discussion about space, calendar, and budget should prevent these struggles.

Realistically, concerns over space, vehicles, volunteers, budget, scheduling, and recognition can lead to competition. One of the commitments that staff members should make is to be concerned with the ministries of others on staff as well as their own personal well-being. Kevin Lawson shares a personal story that illustrates how we often lose sight of our role as team members and need to be reminded of the mutual partnership we share with other staff members:

> I was lovingly confronted one day at a staff meeting when I had finished my agenda items and the associate pastor began to raise some issues in his ministry area. I asked to be excused to get back to work on something,

and he pointed out that he had patiently sat and listened to me discuss my ministry needs many times and that he valued my perspective and input as he wrestled with his. His words brought me up short and gave me a renewed understanding of what it meant to be partners together on a ministry team.[111]

Conclusion

Paul called on the Corinthians to imitate him (1 Cor. 4:16). Ministers have the opportunity to model servant ministry through their relationships with each other and by the way they carry out their responsibilities in their work. Thriving in associate staff ministry contains many variables, but one clear issue is the need to develop godly working relationships with coworkers. Intentional focus on the attitudes affirmed in Scripture and on practical people skills can accomplish much in developing these skills.

Mike Bonem and Roger Patterson use the same concept of thriving in their discussion of second-chair leadership. Deciding to thrive in second-chair leadership (any leader who is not the lead leader) means having an attitude of submission to God and an attitude of a servant in kingdom ministry. Bonem and Patterson also describe someone who thrives in second-chair leadership as one who is thankful for his or her ministry and has passion for being the best in the subordinate role in which he or she has been placed.[112] Keeping in mind Jesus' teaching: "Whoever wants to become great among you must be your servant, and whoever wants to be first must be slave of all" (Mark 10:43-44, NIV), the writers state: "The second chair leader who wants to thrive, personally and organizationally, builds a team by exhibiting a servant's heart....Unlike becoming a team, which requires mutual commitment, your peers cannot prevent you from having a servant's heart or from genuinely offering your support."[113] Cultivating the right attitudes toward one another and practicing practical relationships skills are keys to developing good staff-to-staff relationships.

Review Questions

1. How important are interpersonal relationships to you? What previous experiences influence your concern with interpersonal relationships in the workplace or in ministry?

2. How does the biblical concept of reconciliation speak to the building and maintenance of interpersonal relationships? What is unique about the biblical models of relating to ministry partners?

3. Use the questions under "How well do you get along with others?" in the "Practice Relationship Skills" section to evaluate your practical skills in interpersonal relationships. Identify your areas of strength and areas of weakness.

4. What are some practical ways of spending time together as a staff team that will strengthen interpersonal relationships?

5. What are some areas of struggle that you have observed in relationships among church staff? What biblical texts might speak to the attitudes being displayed?

Suggestions for Further Reading

Mike Bonem and Roger Patterson. *Leading from the Second Chair*. San Francisco, CA: Jossey-Bass, 2005.

Wayne Cordeiro. *Doing Church as a Team*. Ventura, CA: Regal, 2004.

Kevin Lawson. *How to Thrive in Associate Staff Ministry*. Herndon, VA: The Alban Institute, 2000.

Chapter 5

PASTOR AND STAFF TO CONGREGATION RELATIONSHIPS

By Randel Everett, D.Min.

How can the pastor and staff members develop and maintain positive relationships with the congregation? This chapter provides a number of ways to do that.

Learn the Church's Story

When a pastor or staff member begins serving in a new congregation the first thing he or she should do is to learn the church's story. Finding answers to questions like the following can help in doing that:
- When did the church start?
- What was the nature and status of the community when the church began? Was the beginning of the church intentional,

or did the church begin as a split from another congregation? Why was the church started? What were the church's originating values? Have these values changed? Have the demographics of the community shifted? How? Does the church membership reflect the community?

- Who are the heroes of the church both past and present? Why are their lives celebrated? What contributions did they make that have abiding consequences for the church and community? Are they still involved in the church?

- Who are the members who command the respect of the church? Be aware that some people are leaders because of offices they hold, but other leaders have gained the confidence of the congregation through years of faithfulness and wise counsel. When they speak in the halls of the church or in business meetings, the members listen.

- What have been the major contributions of the church to the community? How do folks in the community who are not members of the church describe the church?

- Who are primary ministry partners for the church? Is the congregation involved in the local association of churches? Is the congregation involved in state and national conventions?

- Have previous church leaders been active in ministers' associations or local service organizations? When I was called as the pastor of one church I noticed that membership in the downtown Rotary Club was part of the package. I quickly realized that community involvement was one of the expectations of that church.

- What unique gifts does the church bring to the work of the kingdom? What is the church passionate about? What words quickly surface in conversations? Missions? Christian education? Benevolence?

- What does the church do best? A survey of the local neighborhood will help to identify what the church does well. We did a neighborhood survey in one church in which I served that revealed the church's child development center was the most positive identification of the church by outsiders. Actually the church itself didn't place a lot of value on the school until they began to realize this was a great open door for them in the neighborhood.

- What human resources are available to the church? Churches that are largely blue collar tend to make decisions differently from churches that are primarily white collar. What are the leading professions of members in the church? What are the economic and educational realities of church members? What are their preferences in styles of music?

Churches have stories and personalities just as individuals do. Much of our future is affected by our past. A wise minister will learn as much as possible about a congregation before attempting to lead it. A pastor will ultimately face decisions that may be unpopular with some of the members. Every leader must challenge the status quo if innovations are attempted. The pastor's preaching may stir emotions as congregations are challenged by God's word. By celebrating the successes of a church's past, the pastor increases in effectiveness and creates trust among the church body.

Learn the Church's Community

What are the demographics of the neighborhood? Is the community growing or in decline? What is its ethnic profile?

Are there other churches in the neighborhood? Do the churches participate in shared ministry, community issues, and worship experiences? Are the churches in competition with one another? In my experience all churches benefit when they cooperate. No one congregation has all of the gifts and resources to reach everyone, but churches working together can maximize kingdom effectiveness and meet community needs more completely.

Some communities are positive, growing, and optimistic about the future. Other neighborhoods are in decline and discouraged. Which more clearly reflects the attitude of the community: hopeful, discouraged, depressed, or excited? What are the most apparent needs and resources in the community? Are the people who attend the church primarily from the neighborhood, or do they travel from other locations?

Are there unreached people groups in the ministry area of the church? A people group may be identified by different languages spoken. A people group may also be composed of families with children who have learning differences. A people group may be made up of people who are hearing impaired or who have other unique characteristics.

Within the past two years our West Texas church has had the opportunity to host services for a new Chinn church for immigrants from Myanmar. Their attendance grew to more than 250 before they moved to their own location. We also had the privilege of helping to start a congregation for the hearing impaired. A deaf school was nearby, and yet the families affected by this challenge often found themselves isolated from others.

Describe the Religious Profile of the Community

What religions are prevalent? What percentage of the community identifies itself as having no religious preference? Is the community friendly or hostile to the church?

Pastors should attempt to build relationships with other pastors and even with the leaders of other faith groups. I participate in a panel discussion each year with leaders of other religions, including Muslims, Hindus, Mormons, and Jews. A Catholic priest and I represent the Christian faith. Even though I have faced some criticism for having this dialogue, it gives me an opportunity to make a clear presentation of the gospel to many people who are religious but who know very little about the Christian faith. This exchange of ideas has also encouraged our church members to have religious conversations with coworkers of other faiths.

Our church joins with other churches in shared times of worship. We participate with other Baptist churches through our association. In addition to that, we also share worship on two Sunday nights each year with churches whose racial profile and style of worship is quite different from ours. We have joined with churches of other denominations to host an annual spiritual awakening conference that has brought many of our churches closer together. Our church hosts community Bible study groups for children, youth, and women from our church and from other churches and denominations.

Each church offers a unique contribution to the community. I believe churches and individuals have kingdom assignments. When pastors work together, conflict among church members in the community is reduced. No one church can reach all of the unchurched or meet all ministry needs. However when churches work together, God can accomplish much through them. The unity of the church community creates an environment where the unchurched become open to the gospel.

Define the Mood of the Church

Is the church growing, declining, or maintaining itself? A pastor must not speak unkindly about previous pastors or leadership regardless of the attitude of the church. The pastor should find valuable contributions from the church's history to use as an incentive for future effectiveness.

What is the attitude of the church toward the staff? What is the attitude of the staff toward the congregation?

The pastor is key to developing a healthy relationship between the staff and the congregation. The pastor must consistently speak well of the staff to other members and maintain a positive attitude about the members of the church to the staff. The pastor must communicate to the church that each member of the staff is called. The staff also needs to remember that all of the people of God are called to serve.

A leadership retreat involving key volunteers and staff can be useful for a church to assess its past and plan for the future. At one such retreat we asked the leaders to attempt to define the relevance of the church based on innovations, programs, ministries, buildings, and facilities. What year were the programs begun, and when were the buildings built? Discussing these matters led us to discover that we had fooled ourselves into thinking we were a creative church. We realized that much of our ministry was geared more to previous realities than to the present and the future.

Clarify the Mission of the Church

Too often a church's mission statement may be based on bravado or wishful thinking instead of on a clear recognition of gifts and opportunities. Jim Collins describes the hedgehog concept in his excellent leadership book *Good to Great*.[114] He states that an institution must ask itself three defining questions: *What are we most passionate about? What are we best in the world at? What are our resources?*

A church needs to ask these questions of itself and answer them honestly. The answers must not be based on what we *wish* the church was doing best or what we *believe* our passion should be. Instead we should rigorously attempt to answer frankly. Honest answers can be developed by following up with questions like this: What do others say about us? What

---

Three Defining Questions[115]

- What is the church most passionate about?
- What is the church best at?
- What are the church's resources?

---

are our priorities in the budget and the calendar? What ideas and events bring the most excitement to the congregation?

Key influential leaders in the church, including the pastor and staff, should work on these defining questions together. The mission statement for the church should come from the realities identified by the overlap of these questions.

Implement Best Practices

James Kouzes and Barry Posner have asked the following question to thousands of corporate leaders over the last three decades: *What is the secret to the success of your company?* Their research is the basis of their best-selling book, *The Leadership Challenge.*[116] The empirical evidence they have discovered from their research guided them to best practices that leaders should follow. The following five practices result in exemplary leadership.

Five Practices for Exemplary Leadership[117]
1. Inspire a shared vision
2. Challenge the process
3. Enable others to act
4. Encourage the heart
5. Model the way

1. Inspire a shared vision

A lack of a clearly articulated vision creates leadership gaps, conflicts, and lack of focus within the church. Programs, budgets, and ministries should all show how they are moving the church toward the vision.

The vision must be a shared vision, not just a bold statement by a charismatic leader. It should grow out of the successes of the past, the opportunities of the present, and a sense of the church's unique kingdom opportunity. The vision should be clarified using Jim Collins's hedgehog concept discussed in the previous section, "Clarify the Mission of the Church."

2. Challenge the process

If a church moves from being a good church to a great church, it must challenge the process and the procedures it is following so it will not become complacent. Does the church have the best governance policies? Are the right leaders in the right places? Is the message of the church clearly articulated to the community? Are some of the programs and ministries no longer effective? Can they be celebrated and phased out? What can the church learn from similar churches who have found better ways to accomplish some of the church's ministries?

3. Enable others to act

The words of Ephesians 4:12, "for the equipping of the saints for the work of service, for the building up of the body of Christ" (NASB), remind leaders that they are not responsible for doing all the ministry of the church. Rather, leaders are to equip others to do the work of ministry. This equipping is not done from an ivory tower but by being player-coaches who teach others by walking with them and doing ministry together.

The strength of First Baptist Church of Midland, Texas, where I serve, has been strong lay leadership throughout the history of the church. Pastors and staff have not tried to suppress or silence them but have encouraged them, provided resources, celebrated their contributions, and served alongside them.

4. Encourage the heart

Churches need to celebrate. Of course, we must begin by celebrating the Lord and the Lord's great mercy and grace toward us. But we should also celebrate accomplishments.

Always look for opportunities for recognizing the contributions of others. Through sermons, the church website, and printed publications, tell the stories of the church's effective ministry.

5. Model the way

A pastor cannot lead the staff or the church if the pastor is not practicing what the pastor is preaching. Neither can staff lead a church when the staff's work habits, lifestyles, and relationships give a different message from what they are proclaiming. Jesus told the disciples, "Follow Me" (Mark 1:17, NASB).

Develop a Leadership Council

I received good advice from my dad, who was also a pastor. One thing he said was that when people criticize you, they probably wouldn't if they knew the whole story. But he also said that when people praise you, they probably wouldn't if they knew the whole story. Therefore he advised me to not pay too much attention to either praise or criticism.

Pastors need accountability and encouragement. Jim Collins suggests in his book *Good to Great* that leaders need a leadership council who will help with both of these.[118]

The council should consist of no more than twelve people, and the leader should meet with them regularly. I recommend that the council include key leaders in the church who have the ear of the congregation. They must be wise and not have their own agenda. The council has no authority and does not bring recommendations to the church. However, the pastor meets with them each month for about an hour for fellowship, encouragement, and accountability. A wise pastor will share ideas with this group, especially about sensitive issues in the church or significant decisions the church may face. The council will provide helpful information to the pastor about the concerns, desires, and passions of the congregation.

Create Trust Through Effective Communication

Communication begins with listening. What is the Lord leading the church to be? What are the elders of the church saying about the past and the future? (By elders, I'm not referring to an office in the church but to wise men and women who have been faithful leaders in the church and whose counsel is valued by others.)

Pastors must create an atmosphere of honesty and openness with staff. The staff should follow this example with the congregation.

The pastor and the staff must be accessible to the church. A pastor should never surprise the church or the staff. Sensitive issues should be discussed with key people before being shared more publicly. Weekly staff meetings are essential for ministry staff.

The pastor should plan monthly meetings (often around breakfast or coffee) with key lay leaders, such as the chair of deacons and the chair of the church council. The purpose of the meeting is for the strengthening of relationships, but it also will provide a great opportunity for discussion and input.

Follow Church Policies

What is the pastor's role in decision making? What is the role of the staff? What is the role of the committees? What requires church action? How can grassroots input be received for large decisions like the budget, construction projects, and ministry partnerships? How can business decisions be effective and efficient? Effective governance policies can help in answering such questions.

Too many churches have governance policies that make it difficult to move forward. Church policies should be reviewed every four or five years by the staff and lay leadership to ensure they are effective and efficient.

How can decisions be effectively communicated to the congregation? Staff, committees, and the congregation need to receive adequate information and sufficient time before they are asked to make a decision. When decisions are made, they must be communicated effectively to the church.

Maintain a Good Reputation in the Community

Pastors and the staff should be involved in community activities to learn more of the needs and opportunities of the community and also to bring the hope of Christ to them. A church should identify other churches and ministry partners for shared opportunities for worship, training, and outreach. Pastors should build relationships with other pastors. Church members should be encouraged to participate in the activities of government, education, foundations, sports, and other community events and organizations.

Use Grace and Gratitude When Beginning and Ending a Ministry

When beginning a ministry, be gracious to predecessors and celebrate the church's heritage (see the first section, "Learn the Church's Story"). When leaving a congregation, be thoughtful of your decision's impact on others. Inform key staff, church leaders, and close friends privately before a public decision is announced. Use gracious speech in announcing a decision, and utilize appropriate public venues (pulpit, church newsletter, website, etc.).

Allow an appropriate period of time before leaving so the church can be ready for the period of transition. However, don't stay too long after you have announced that you are leaving. Staying too long creates an awkwardness for the church and one's family. Be sure that relationships and responsibilities are in good standing to the best of your ability before you leave.

God is gracious to those of us who have been called as pastors and staff members for God's church. It is a privilege and a trust we have received from God. Things are not always easy, and at times the hard work and contributions of leaders goes without recognition. However, our work must be done unto the Lord.

A Scripture passage that helps me to clarify my focus is Hebrews 12:1-3, which reads as follows:

> "Therefore, since we have so great a cloud of witnesses surrounding us, let us also lay aside every encumbrance and the sin which so easily entangles us, and let us run with endurance the race that is set before us, fixing our eyes on Jesus, the author and perfecter of faith, who for the joy set before Him endured the cross, despising the shame, and has sat down at the right hand of the throne of God. For consider Him who has endured such hostility by sinners against Himself, so that you will not grow weary and lose heart" (NASB).

Review Questions

1. Which three ways for the pastor and staff to develop and maintain positive relationships with the congregation seem most promising to you?

2. Which three ways for the pastor and staff to develop and maintain positive relationships with the congregation seem most challenging to you?

3. Focus on one of the ways for the pastor and staff to develop and maintain positive relationships with the congregation, and develop an action plan for implementing it in a place of ministry with which you are familiar.

Suggestions for Further Reading

Jim Collins. *Good to Great: Why Some Companies Make the Leap . . . And Others Don't.* New York: HarperBusiness, 2001.

James M. Kouzes and Barry Z. Posner. *The Leadership Challenge: How to Make Extraordinary Things Happen in Organizations.* Fifth edition. San Francisco: Jossey-Bass, 2012.

Chapter 6

DEVELOPING GOOD CONGREGATION-TO-STAFF RELATIONSHIPS

By Bill Brian, J.D.

> "Appreciate your pastoral leaders who gave you the Word of God. Take a good look at the way they live, and let their faithfulness instruct you, as well as their truthfulness" (Hebrews 13:7, *The Message*).

The church is an autonomous body, operating through democratic processes under the lordship of Jesus Christ.[119] We sing the hymn, "The church's one foundation is Jesus Christ, her Lord."[120] In one of the two times Jesus used the word "church," Jesus described the pattern for resolving differences among members of a local congregation of believers (Matthew 18:15–17).

With Christ as the cornerstone for every local congregation, and with this guide for repairing relationships coming directly from our Savior's lips, the model for sound relationships in every church is set before us in the New Testament in the Acts of the Apostles and in the Letters of Paul, Peter, James, John, and Jude.

Church members loving one another, regarding others as better than themselves, leading by serving, exercising discipline with humility, embracing believers from every nation, giving of material resources as God has prospered—all of these undergird the healthy relationship between staff and congregation. A "healthy" relationship is robust, sound, whole, wholesome, strong, and free from weakness and disease.

The primary methodology in this chapter for exploring guides to good relationships among congregation and staff is a survey conducted among six Baptist churches in Texas, all affiliated with the Baptist General Convention of Texas. The pastor and two laypeople from each church, selected by the pastor, were asked to respond to questions bearing on healthy congregation/staff relationships. In the interest of obtaining the greatest degree of candor in the responses, each pastor was promised anonymity regarding both the name of the church and the respondent. In four out of the six churches, the present pastors have served more than ten years—in one case more than twenty years. In two churches, the pastors have served fewer than five years, but they serve congregations where pastoral tenure is far more than the average of two years.[121]

In the survey, the pastor was asked to respond to specific questions and was, in turn, asked to enlist one or two lay members of the congregation to respond to questions about the pastor search and the ongoing process of staff/congregation relations. The author is most grateful for candid, thoughtful, and thorough responses. A few additional sources were writings and oral comments received by the author from pastors and laypeople over the years.

The Pastor Search Process

Preceding the establishment of a healthy relationship between congregation and pastor (and staff) is, of course, the process of searching for a pastor. The pastor search process varies greatly from church to church, and as one respondent to the survey observed, "No two search processes within the same church are identical."

What do successful pastor searches have in common? These commonalities are not simply those that result in the call of a pastor; rather, they result in the call of a pastor whose pastorate is marked by a long tenure, harmony within the church, and a sense that the Lord is leading the congregation.

What underlies the best pastor search processes? Three essentials emerged from the survey: a clear understanding of the character of the church; prayer; and effective communication.

Calling a pastor who regards himself as the ruler of the church to a congregation whose history testifies to servant leadership with shared responsibilities by the pastor and members will present a difficult challenge for both the church and the new pastor. Understanding a church's identity defines the kind of person who will be the best fit for the congregation. Is the church a new congregation or one that has existed for decades? What is its history? What personality traits marked the former pastors? What did they accomplish with the church? How were they regarded by the community? by the Baptist denomination? How does the church spend most of its budget? How is it governed—by the deacon body, by committees, or by an authoritative pastor?

The congregation and the search committee should take the time to reflect on who they are. This time might include the committee reaching out to the congregation to determine what the congregation is looking for in a new pastor, a part of documenting the character of this particular church.

The congregation and the search committee should spend time to reflect on who they are.

Prayer by the committee, the congregation, and the candidate is a second key. One lay respondent remembered "the amount of time spent in prayer...as a group and as individuals," even though the search happened more than twenty years ago. Another respondent concurred, "The search committee had a strong commitment to prayer." Instead of beginning with the preparation of a profile of the next pastor, the committee had a prayer retreat. Each time they met, they spent at least an hour praying together. The pastor of this congregation explained that he asked the committee to stay together for the first year after the church called him to continue to meet for monthly prayer. One pastoral candidate recalled that God worked through the search committee and the candidate's own prayer partner in another city.

Prayer by the committee, congregation, and candidate is the second key.

Third, effective communication is a commonality among successful pastoral searches. Effective communication begins with the selection of the search committee itself. One respondent recalled that the selection of the committee had been an open process. The selection of that church's search committee of seven, with two alternates, was accomplished by written nominations from church members. The seven members and two alternates earning the most nominations were presented for congregational affirmation. To be included, nominees were required to be tithers. Nominee names, moreover, were submitted to the church family for approval as a whole slate. A majority of *no* votes would have required the review and submission of an entirely new group of proposed search committee members and alternates for the church to consider. Seeking a diverse committee, another church gave consideration to age, gender, years as a church member, and areas of service as qualifications to serve on the pastor search committee.

Third, effective communication is a commonality among successful pastoral searches.

One pastor recalled that communication by the search committee was clear, consistent, and appropriate. The candidate was always informed as to where he stood in the search process. The pastor recalled that the committee worked well through a single spokesperson, its chairman, so that the candidate did not receive competing and confusing calls from the various committee members.

The search committee should also keep the congregation informed about the committee's process through regular communication, sometimes orally during the worship service or in church business conference, at other times through written communication in the church's regularly published newsletter, on the church's website, or in other communication media. Of course, due regard for the confidentiality of candidate names means that not all details can be shared with the congregation at all stages of the search process.

Respecting confidentiality recognizes the importance of the relationship between the pastoral candidate and the pastor's current congregation (not the congregation conducting the search) and is most essential to finding the best candidate for the church. If the candidate is fearful of botched confidentiality, the candidate may dismiss the search early on. Breaches of confidentiality do great harm to the search process in numerous ways. If it becomes apparent that communication leaks are occurring from among the committee, candid discussions are impaired, trust erodes, suspicions arise, and harmony wanes. Equally important, consideration and respect must be shown to the church where a potential candidate is presently serving. Should the process end with a candidate, the candidate must be able to continue to serve effectively in his present congregation.

One pastor recalls the coordination of timing the announcement of the call in the new congregation with giving the pastor the permission to tell his existing congregation of that call. This coordination of timing was done in a way that caused the least amount of damage to the candidate's current church. This same pastor recalled that he was given access to the new congregation at the appropriate time so that he and the church family could communicate in a churchwide open forum. Two pastor respondents recalled opportunities to meet with church staff members in the new congregation. One pastor recalled having had the opportunity to spend at least thirty minutes with each key staff person in the new congregation, an opportunity that was very important to that candidate.

No substitute exists for thoroughness in the due diligence of reference checks. Every candidate should give references. The committee should inquire not only of each of those references, but also ask that the furnished reference, in turn, give further references. These "second-level" references should also be checked to gain additional insights. The tedious but essential work of checking references should be done with a single questionnaire, ensuring that the same basic questions are asked of each reference. The task of checking references can be divided among search committee members so that no one committee member is overburdened.

Search committee sizes ranged from five members to fourteen among the churches surveyed. The number of committee members should be sufficient enough to reflect the diverse makeup of the congregation. While a larger committee permits the delegation of responsibilities to be shared among more committee members, a smaller committee might serve more efficiently with a greater expectation of confidentiality.

Reflecting on the search process, one pastor recalled that he had been involved in simultaneous processes with two different churches in two different states. He recalled that one congregation was ready to hire him "sight unseen," sending the minister of music from that congregation to hear a sample sermon. This pastor observed, "The process seemed somewhat odd and frightening." Another pastor recalled being voted on four times during the process, which he called "stressful." Two respondents got the impression that the new congregation would like to hire as cheaply as possible (trying to "lowball" the compensation).

One pastor recalled that honest, candid discussions about the church and its leadership are vital, with no secrets or surprises, with time to pray, and with calm and steady leadership from the committee chair and vice-chair. One pastor reported with great favor that the committee invited him to ask a question of the committee before the committee began asking its questions of him. One church's questionnaire for the pastor included multiple objective and subjective inquiries, covering theology, leadership style, and personal conduct of the candidate, with page after page of questions during a lengthy interview process. Additionally, an understanding of questions that the candidate's spouse might have and respect for the spouse's own personality, ministry gifts, and place in the new church family mark a mature, balanced search process. Giving the spouse opportunity to ask questions and introducing the spouse to a new city show tenderness and regard for the candidate's family.

One could easily see that a mismatch of congregation expectations and candidate expectations could make for a difficult time for both church and pastor. Put another way, one pastor respondent observed, "One of the worst faults of most search committees is poor communication with candidates."

In summary, the committee should view itself as a communication link between the congregation and the candidate. The committee should not seek a candidate other than one whom the committee honestly believes will be the best fit for the congregation. The committee should try to put itself in the shoes of the candidate, having due regard for confidentiality and questions the candidate will have about the prospective new church. And although the committee must be thorough enough to know who it is they will recommend to the congregation, respect should always be shown for the candidate's present congregation.

Transition to the New Congregation

What happens after the church has called a new pastor? Is there any continuing role for the pastor search committee? What steps can a congregation take to help the new pastor begin an effective ministry?

Although the search committee has completed its official assignment when a pastor has been called, the calling church should recognize that the faces of the search committee members are the ones most familiar to the new pastor. Continued presence and support of committee members are essential and are a blessing to a new pastor. A search committee, having recommended a candidate who is elected by the congregation—even if the committee's vote was not unanimous—must present the unified voice of the committee, with no formal or informal "minority" report.

Observations by surveyed pastors are most helpful in understanding how best to transition the new pastor to the new congregation. One respondent said that the new pastor must know his own "kingdom assignment." He must know who he is, what he does best, and what he is passionate about. The new pastor also needs to become very much acquainted with the history and accomplishments of the new church. The new pastor should become familiar with the community and should begin building relationships with key staff and lay leadership at once. Further, the new pastor must have the prayer support of persons who will pray earnestly and faithfully for the new pastor and family. The former search committee is a natural choice for this initial prayer support.

One pastor experienced the benefits of a transition team of lay leaders. The lesson from this experience is that the church should provide adequate resources to help the new pastor's family make the move and get settled during the exciting, yet nervous, days of transition.

Much was said in the surveys about managing the demands of every constituency of the new congregation. A good balance needs to be found—giving the pastor and people opportunities to have adequate contact but without overloading the new pastor with too many events too quickly. One church identified a staff member, former pastor, or deacon to take the new pastor on the initial hospital rounds, introducing the new pastor to administrators and chaplains. Also, it is useful to introduce the new pastor to the local Baptist association director of missions to gain an understanding of the role of the new church in that association. In one church, the new pastor made personal, one-on-one visits with the oldest members of the congregation to gain knowledge of the history of the church. This same pastor asked members to send him their favorite Scriptures, on which he based a number of his early sermons. In another congregation, the new pastor's strong work ethic and shepherding spirit quickly endeared him to the congregation.

The new pastor must not try to be an imitation of the previous pastor. When he retired, one wise pastor told the congregation, "If you don't let the new pastor be his own man, I'll come back to haunt you."

Calling a pastor who is a good fit for the congregation includes an understanding of the role the congregation expects from its pastor. Does the church have a history of asking the pastor primarily to preach? Is the pastor directly involved in the day-to-day church administration? Does the pastor officiate at funerals and weddings, or do other staff members take most of these assignments?

Preexisting personnel issues often frustrate the transition process for the new pastor. When issues cannot be resolved before the new pastor arrives, inform the candidate of these issues at the appropriate stage of the search process. The search committee should do all it can to keep the new pastor from being blindsided by lurking surprises.

One pastor cited meeting with key interest groups and staff members and engaging in give-and-take with committees on key issues as being useful. In another church, all the staff members were honored by the church within one month after the new pastor arrived. Each staff member was given a nice gift, modestly priced but personalized according to each one's interests. That pastor remembered, "It made us all feel valued/appreciated."

The committee should include the pastor's spouse at critical, appropriate junctures of the search and transition processes. However, the committee should not presume on the time or interests of the pastor's spouse. The pastor's spouse should have the opportunity and freedom to make choices of places to serve based on personal interests.

What Is the Foundation for a Healthy Relationship Between Staff and Congregation?

Among the six churches surveyed, a sign of good health was a unified core. Lay leaders and pastors alike said that good communication is at the heart of a healthy relationship between congregation and staff. Communication includes understanding "the church's *DNA*," as one pastor responded. What is the church known for doing well (Sunday School, missions, benevolence, worship)? What is this congregation passionate about? Who are the church's primary ministry and mission partners (local association, state convention, Southern Baptist Convention, Cooperative Baptist Fellowship)?

᷍᷍

Lay leaders and pastors alike said that good communication is at the heart of a healthy relationship between congregation and staff.

⌒

A review of the pastors' responses reveals a consensus that the pastor must accept much of the responsibility for healthy relationships between congregation and staff. As one pastor commented, "The church generally takes their cue from us." Trust between congregation and staff, born of genuine love rooted in the New Testament, is essential. Of this trust, one pastor noted, "[This] church has loved and trusted us in ways that give life to me and my family." The personnel committee chairperson in that same church concluded that the foundation to a healthy relationship between church and staff is "trust, mutual respect, and inclusion." This lay member expanded on the subject of trust and respect:

> Trust and respect are built, in part, through familiarity and friendship that grows over time, and [this] church's pastors and called staff have generally been long tenured. [The current pastor] and the current called staff members have not only performed their roles very well and with a high degree of integrity, they have also become friends and family to [this] church congregation over the years. They are connecting and regularly making themselves visible and accessible. They are also highly respected.

This same member observed that the committee-run polity in that church lends itself to mutual respect, trust, transparency, and congregational inclusion related to the church's business and direction.[122]

One pastor-respondent said, "While my answer may not be popular, the reality is no one can save the pastor from himself. There is no deacon chairman or personnel committee member who can create humility in a pastor who is arrogant."

The church staff must clearly understand the church's expectations for them. The pastor is key to the bridge between congregation and staff. The pastor should communicate expectations of the church to the staff and should communicate the ministries of the staff to the congregation. The church should have clarity about its own polity. What is the role of the pastor? What is the role of staff? Are the deacons a decision-making, governing body? What is the role of church committees? Does the church have a council? If so, what is its role? The staff must understand church procedures for decision making and communicate to the congregation clearly that those procedures are being followed.

Also, the staff must understand the community they serve. Where are the greatest needs and opportunities? This idea of "community" includes both the congregation itself and the city and region where that church is located.

When it comes to staff members other than the pastor, the pastor plays a role, along with the personnel committee, in making sure that expectations, successes, and failures are noted and addressed. While the pastor and staff hear many different, even contradictory, voices from the same congregation, someone has to help the staff member find a central voice. One pastor said, "I often will tell my staff members that I have many bosses (approximately 5,000), but they have only one—me."

Another pastor noted the shared responsibility between congregation and staff. "If one or the other recognizes that the relationship is strained for any reason, biblically they are encouraged to take the initiative in seeking to mend the rift." Staff retreats afford an opportunity to address healthy relationships among the church staff.

The pastor should not be jealous of the successes of other staff members. One pastor said, "No one in the congregation is happier than I when a staff member is praised by the congregation. It makes me look good, too."

A lay respondent noted that while the role of staff is clearly one of leadership, it is not leading the congregation to become a reflection of the pastor; rather, it is leadership based primarily in service. Staff can help the congregation discern its identity, both what it is and what it can become. One personnel committee chairperson pointed to a right understanding of the scriptural role of the church in the world. In this context, proper behavior by staff and congregation encompasses mutually kind, forgiving personal relationships, salt and light attitudes, mutual love, and respect.

What Can the Personnel Committee Do to Maintain a Healthy Relationship Between Congregation and Staff?

Although the survey consensus was that good relationships between congregation and staff start with the pastor, all respondents recognized an important role for the personnel committee. The personnel committee is a link between the congregation and the staff that is best served by the ability to exchange and process confidential information. Setting appropriate compensation, reviewing job performance, and setting policy among church staff are key functions of the personnel committee.

Committees will function in different ways, depending on the tradition that exists within the church, the leadership style of the pastor, and the role of deacons in the church. In one congregation, a former personnel committee member noted that the pastor is a hands-on pastor, but not autocratic. That pastor seeks the committee's input on personnel decisions and exhibits a view of the roles of the pastor, committee, and congregation in those decisions that is both proper and consistent with that congregation's "way of doing things."

The committee can assist the congregation in maintaining a healthy relationship by providing honest, straightforward communication between committee and pastor, support for the pastoral role while consistently searching for ways properly to recognize and compensate, and support for the entire staff. In one congregation, the committee's primary roles are working with the pastor to bring qualified ministerial staff members to the church as necessary, ensuring that the allocation of staff responsibilities matches the needs of the congregation, and making certain that staff members are properly compensated.

In one church the committee conducts a thorough evaluation of all staff members to maintain accountability and satisfactory job performance. In that congregation, the personnel committee provides regular, periodic reports to the deacon body and congregation concerning activities of the various ministries of the church. The committee has a diverse membership (recommended by a committee on committees) and provides continuous feedback to the pastor from the perspective of lay members of the congregation concerning staff leadership and job performance.

In another congregation, the senior pastor relates mostly to deacons and deacon officers. In that church, the associate pastor communicates most with the personnel committee. In yet another congregation, the personnel committee, together with the deacon body, provides the primary feedback and communication between the pastor and the congregation. Another church adopted a "pray with our pastor" time to enable deacons to join with the pastor on a weekly basis to pray for the church and its members. In every model of shared leadership, respondents to the survey found continuous, good communication vital to healthy staff-congregation relations.

The personnel committee can administer service milestone recognitions for pastor and staff. In one congregation, the benefits associated with staff service milestones are detailed in the church's personnel policies and include varying combinations of monetary gifts and special recognition in church publications (or its web page) and worship services. That church has a sabbatical policy granted to the pastor and ministerial staff members at certain intervals of service. These sabbaticals are designed to enhance the ministries and the effectiveness of staff members with the congregation. The personnel committee is also that congregation's designated body to approve competitive compensation and benefits programs for all staff and to express tangible appreciation for staff service.

The personnel committee in one church meets on an as-needed (if irregular) basis. The pastor (and the staff coordinator, for positions under the staff coordinator's supervision) recommends a candidate to fill a staff ministry position. By this point in the process, the potential staff member has already been thoroughly researched. The committee knows that the pastor would not bring a name without having done much "homework." The final recommendation to the congregation, nonetheless, comes from the committee once it has also interviewed the candidate. In that church, each year the pastor also brings to the committee proposals for staff compensation (other than the pastor's). Again, the committee knows that much study has gone into the proposals, including a periodic confidential survey of salaries from similarly situated churches. All salary information, after being reviewed by the committee, is returned to the pastor. The committee does its own research and recommends (in the pastor's absence) the pastor's compensation review and proposal. In that church, the pastor reports to the personnel committee on recommendations to recognize, along with the congregation, staff members' milestone anniversaries.

What Pastors Wish Lay Members of the Congregation Knew

Each pastor was asked, "What do you wish the key lay leaders in your congregation knew (but you fear that they don't know) that would strengthen the relationship between congregation and staff?" The pastors' responses to this question were more diverse than to any other question in the survey.

One pastor noted that negativity and complaining do not strengthen the bonds between congregation and staff. He said, "Leaders on staff and...lay leaders must pray for each other and believe that God is working. We can trust the truth spoken in love."

One pastor cited "trusting the staff" as something he wished key lay leaders would do. That pastor recognized the growing distrust of institutions and leadership in our culture generally. He noted that the congregation needs to remember that the ministerial staff and the pastor are called by God and by the congregation and to recognize that the staff members have received unique preparation and training for their positions, borne out by their competence, work ethic, and commitment to Christ and the church as they work alongside lay leaders.

"Recognize the staff's burdens and responsibilities," said one pastor, who added, "Understand the unique challenges the families of staff members face. It's often more difficult to be a spouse or child of a minister than it is to be the minister."

In one church, the pastor's call to ministry sometimes conflicts with the daily maintenance of the church. This pastor said that he and his peers find themselves sometimes in the role of being CEOs of religious institutions. "We felt called to lead and equip the saints to do ministry, but we find ourselves having to manage large non-profit 'businesses.'" This tension can erode a pastor's heart and passion.

For the congregation to permit the pastor to experience God and receive grace, the people must understand that the church is where both they and the staff work and worship. One pastor noted, "We are better pastors when we are allowed to be church members as well as leaders. This is true for our families as well." In this same vein, another pastor remembered a telephone call to the church on the Thursday before Easter. A church member had died; the church offices would be closed on Good Friday, but the family wanted the funeral on Saturday. This pastor wrote, "It's Thursday, the church is closed tomorrow, but one way or another we have to make it happen. This is the daily life and grind."

One pastor wished that church members understood that neither the pastor nor the staff can know about a hospitalization, a job layoff, or a death in a church member's family unless the church is notified: "The pastor and staff are not mind readers."

Also, the pet projects of lay leaders are not necessarily part of the mission of the whole church. They should not expect the pastor and staff to sponsor, promote, or participate in the members' own pet projects.

ᘓ

"Nothing strengthens the relationship of congregation to staff more than each knowing that the other values/loves them."

ᘓ

For lay leaders to understand the time invested by church staff members and appreciate the excellence in ministry that is offered is vital to sustaining staff ministries. Said one pastor, "Nothing strengthens the relationship of congregation to staff more than each knowing that the other values/loves them."

Conclusion

The path to a healthy, robust relationship between the staff and the congregation as a whole begins with a search process for a pastor who recognizes the history and character of the church making the call and that earnestly seeks the best match between church and pastor. Once a pastor is called, support and encouragement, coupled with mutually respectful visiting sessions to get to know the people, help the new pastor and his family transition to a healthy and effective ministry experience.

Although the pastor is the key to a healthy relationship between congregation and staff, the lay leadership (personnel committee, deacon body, or church council) must work with the pastor and ministerial staff to attend to expectations, successes, and mistakes and bring proper and regular recognition for staff service milestone anniversaries that permit the church and staff to join in celebration of God's goodness to his people.

Foundational to all of these components is prayer by pastor, staff, and lay members, seasoned with humility on the part of all in the spirit of Paul's charge to the believers at Philippi: "In humility consider others better than yourselves. Each of you should look not only to your own interests, but also to the interests of others" (Philippians 2:3–4, NIV84). Finally, free-flowing, consistent, and continuous appropriate communication among pastor, staff, and congregation, speaking the truth in love, builds trust and respect for both congregation and staff.

One pastor's young adult daughter had told him, "I just love our church, Daddy. They sure do take good care of us." He remarked, "While so many ministers' children grow up resenting the church, mine have grown up loving the...church. Every pastor can only hope that his children would see the good in God's people by the way they treat their pastor." How much would every lay leader in a Baptist church thrill to hear what that pastor shared.

Review Questions

1. Where do we find the model for sound relationships within the church?

2. What do we mean when we speak of the "polity" of a church?

3. How can a church determine its character?

4. What is the role of confidentiality in (a) the successful search for a pastor or other staff member and (b) the ongoing

process of building and maintaining a healthy relationship between congregation and staff?

5. If there is any one person who holds the key to congregation/staff relations, who is it?

Chapter 7

CHRISTIAN ETHICS IN CHURCH RELATIONSHIPS

Larry C. Ashlock, Ph.D., and William M. Tillman, Ph.D.

PART A

PRACTICING CHRISTIAN ETHICS IN PASTOR, STAFF, AND CONGREGATIONAL RELATIONSHIPS

Larry C. Ashlock, Ph.D.

"The view was incredible" is a statement that often is used to describe the visual appeal of a particular destination. One of the distinct privileges of my life has been the opportunity to travel to some of the most beautiful settings on earth—the majestic Nile River in Uganda; the snow-capped mountains that ring Santiago, Chile; and the misty, windswept hills of Wales. These scenes all led me to say, "The view was incredible!" The appraisal of any view, however, depends on one's judgment; and what is true of geography also finds its parallel in relationships. Indeed, the oft-repeated cliché, "Beauty is in the eye of the beholder," applies ethically because not all interactions a pastor, staff, and congregation experience in their relationships are viewed the same way by each category of participants. One's view of the moral quality of church staff relationships often depends on the vantage point.

Defining Christian Ethics in the Church and Staff Context

What Is Christian Ethics?

Ethics is "the discipline dealing with what is good and bad or right and wrong or with moral duty and obligation."[123] Every day we face decisions about how we should live; hence, ethics involves choices. Human beings live as people who have a sense of right and wrong, better and worse. Humankind tries to distinguish between good and evil, give reasons for such distinctions, and then act accordingly. Somehow people know that what they do matters. However, there is a distinct difference in the meaning of ethics when the focus becomes *Christian* ethics. Christians know that character and choices *matter to God*. Such a claim, however, is easier stated than it is acted upon.

Numerous Approaches to Ethics

To begin with, there would seem to be as many approaches to ethics as there are people. Until recently such a subject was often left for discussions in academic settings. Contemporary ethics has brought the subject into the cultural mainstream and includes emphases like virtue, freedom from oppression, and right ends.[124] The subject of ethics is often complex and nuanced, but for Christians, God's character and way remains the ultimate source of all that is right and good. Postmoderns have grown accustomed to basing authority, as well as rights and justice claims, in constitutions or in nature (human), but the Scriptures teach that all authority is God's. All that is right and just stems from God's nature and will.

Secondly, *clergy ethics* as a category has often been subsumed under broader areas like professional ethics, causing a lack of clarity about the specific nature and application of ministry ethics. Even though there are similarities between ministry and professions like medicine and law, professional models do not readily fit ministry.[125] Most would view the responsibility to lead a congregation as a unique office under Christ's authority—a *calling*.[126] Indeed, all Christians are *called*; yet, in the case of ministry, some are set apart by the congregation through ordination to see that the church remains true to its gospel mission. This office is an ethical enterprise precisely because it represents God and involves relationships with people. Therefore, a minister's character and actions hold ethical implications in church life.

Ethical Implications of Relationships

Pastor-Staff Relationships

An ethical issue that underlies pastor-staff relationships relates to a fault line that often exists between the *servant* and *shepherd* leadership motifs. Pastors and staff members typically emphasize *diakonia*, or servanthood, but conflict can emerge whenever a pastor assumes a shepherding role that becomes more *directing*.[127] The latter approach to pastoral staff relationships is grounded in the application of authority in ways that confuse and, at times, bruise staff members. In reality, although we often state that ministers are *equal*, we do not clearly (or carefully) establish links that integrate parity with pastoral supervision. Like oil and water, the two concepts and applications sometimes do not readily mix. Space does not permit an extensive examination of the supervisory pastor-staff relationship, but certainly both pastors and staff members should respect human dignity (sanctity of life), seek to maintain a healthy balance between individual freedom and responsibilities (rights),[128] and strive for fairness (justice).[129]

Ethical staff relationships are rooted in *God's ultimate authority* and stem from a desire by a pastor and staff members to honor God's will in all interactions. When a pastor and staff model *collegiality* and *partnering,* they practice relationships that enhance human dignity.[130] This approach to ministry demonstrates good theology as well, because this social aspect to ministry is rooted in a symbol, "God is love" (1 John 4:8, 16, NASB). God models this emblem in the Trinity. He is "eternally the giver or lover (Father), the receiver or beloved (Son), and the gift or love which binds them together (Spirit)."[131] The doctrine of the Trinity teaches us self-giving relationships. We have been created to share and are unable to enhance "dignity" apart from being in relationships and "sharing our gifts for the sake of each other and the whole community."[132]

Respect for freedom, equality, and human rights is an outgrowth of our understanding of being fashioned in God's image (see Genesis 1:26–27; 9:6). Whereas laws made by humans aim to protect humans, many pastor-staff and staff-church relationships, sadly, do not reflect God's creation law and do not protect humans. Practically stated, regardless of job titles or roles, people are intended to be treated as *ends* rather than used as *means to an end*.[133]

As a result, pastors and staff members, by virtue of their common humanity as God's creations, are free to pursue justice in relationships with each other. A pastor's goal should be to protect the vulnerable. Two ethical principles emerge from within this moral obligation to protect those over whom we exercise authority and power—beneficence/nonmaleficence and trust. The Hippocratic physician was exhorted to do good, or at least to do no harm, to a patient. Likewise, pastors and staff members do well to practice both beneficence and nonmaleficence in relationships with one another. This means that those in authority have a responsibility to work for the good of those they supervise, not for their harm. Secondly, the ethical principle of trust/trustworthiness implies that a pastor will not abuse the power that comes by virtue of the pastor's influence over others. Whether the issue is sexual misconduct, divulging confidential information, or simply truth-telling, the pastor's influence must be used for good, not harm. These core ethical principles apply equally to the wider circle of relationships that pastors have with others.

Pastor-Congregation Relationships

Few, if any, ethical concerns are more critical than a *pastor and power*. A pastor can abuse power and wound associates. The same holds true for congregational relationships. Space here does not permit an exhaustive examination of power, but several highlights may be stated. Everything a pastor does to meet the needs of others flows through pastoral relationships. It is critical that a pastor accept being trustworthy as a moral imperative. This is termed a pastor's "fiduciary responsibility," which means that a pastor will use power and authority in ways that will serve the needs of those who seek his or her pastoral service. A pastor will not exploit the vulnerabilities of congregants but instead will give greater preference to their best interests.[134] Pastors will respect all that church members entrust to them.

Few, if any, ethical concerns are more critical than a pastor and power.

A pastor's ethical responsibility to church members regularly surfaces in two key relationships. *Counseling* relationships, by their nature, include some level of secrecy. Clergy confidentiality protects the power that an individual normally exerts over himself or herself. A pastor will keep the interest of the congregant foremost in mind when in a counseling relationship. For example, confidentiality means that a pastor will shun the sharing of a pastoral concern that is gained in a private counseling session with others.[135] Secondly, *sexuality* is a fundamental component of personality. Through our human sexuality we relate to self, others, the world, and even God. Sexuality contains both "a promise and a peril." It is a "promise" because our sexuality is a relational power that, among other things, enables us to be "tenderly present" to others.[136] This empathy holds the "promise" that God can use us individually to help others. Inherent also in our sexuality is the peril that it can become an instrument of abuse, exploitation, and disorder.[137] Sexual misconduct is a misuse of pastoral power and a betrayal of trust. Such behavior by a pastor, responsible to God for the care of souls, uses persons who lack the ability or the will to protect themselves from sexual stimulation.[138] Sexual abuse includes the exploitation of children, women, disabled individuals, and the elderly.[139] The misuse and abuse of sexuality by a pastor includes using one's personal, professional, or physical power to develop a romantic relationship with someone under his or her care, or to use a person for one's own sexual stimulation or satisfaction.[140] Pastoral moral responsibility is not only a concern of the local church; it also extends to the wider community of church relationships.

Relating Ethically to Pastors and Staff Members of Other Congregations

One of the tragic facts of the sinking of the luxury cruise ship *Titanic* was the horrifying truth that some of those safely inside lifeboats refused to offer assistance to others who were drowning in the icy Atlantic. An often unspoken truth (but a hard reality of contemporary ministry) is the lack of genuine community (*koinonia*) demonstrated between pastors and staff members of different congregations. Exercising ethical leadership with regard to other pastors and church staff members means that a pastor will also employ the same trio of holistic moral duties in these relationships—respect for human dignity, respect for individual and corporate rights, and the practice of justice.

Since we are all created in God's image, pastors will treat pastors and staff members in other congregations with respect, refusing to speak derisively about their colleagues in ministry.

Since we are all created in God's image, pastors will treat pastors and staff members in other congregations with respect, refusing to speak derisively about their colleagues in ministry. There is a mutuality of obligation to love other believers because all have been fashioned in Christ's image. Respect for the rights of those in other congregations will mean that pastors will avoid *sheep stealing*, or soliciting members from other churches. Too often, smaller churches are treated somewhat like *farm clubs* in relationship to major league baseball organizations. Pastors of small congregations love and nurture their members only to see them *called up* to a competing church. Christian justice extends well beyond the secular variety because it is rooted in the love of Christ. True justice is not based solely on some calculus of what is owed to another; it is what is called forth by love.[141] A titanic failure in church relationships occurs when love of self (and one's own church) eclipses love of others and other ministries. Christlike justice requires that pastors will take the lead in modeling genuine care for the poor, the weak, and the troubled in all the congregations around them.

Summary

A pastor's relationships with staff members, members of the congregation, and other pastors and churches bear deep ethical implications. The pastor serves as a vital conduit of God's love in the lives of those he has been called to serve. Holistic concern for the lives of individuals promotes health and wellness in the body of Christ. Indeed, the quality of the relationship is based in part on the view of the pastor, but this is not the only view in question. Staff members bear the responsibility to reciprocate in ways that affirm a pastor's dignity, rights, and claims to justice.

Review Questions

1. What are some of the contributing factors to pastor-staff conflict in your particular church context? Design a biblical approach to better link staff parity with pastoral supervision.

2. What biblical core values are adversely impacted when there is a rivalry between the leaders of two different congregations? Design a strategy to improve pastor-to-pastor and staff-to-staff relationships that is rooted in biblical core values.

Suggestions for Further Reading

In addition to the books cited in the endnotes, consider these books:
Henry Blackaby and Richard Blackaby. *Spiritual Leadership: Moving People on to God's Agenda*. Nashville: B & H Books, rev. ed., 2011.
Brother Lawrence. *The Practice of the Presence of God.*

PART B

THE CONGREGATION RELATING ETHICALLY TO THE PASTOR, STAFF, AND OTHER CONGREGATIONS

By William M. Tillman, Ph.D.

The story is told about congregants who visited their pastor, who was hospitalized. One of the church members said, "We have come to report a vote at the church—203 to 157—that you get well."

Generally, this joke, and many like it, get a giggle—which implies a lightness to the conversation. We must realize humor is a powerful mechanism, however, for carrying the energy of transcending incongruent ideas. At the heart of this joke is one scenario depicting how church staff and members relate to one another. The not-so-beneath the surface message is that church staff and church members can quite often live in adversarial contexts.

Bill Wilson of the Center of Congregational Health astutely outlines such contexts:

What about the ongoing question of whether a congregation is to be **staff-led** or **lay-led?**

...[C]hoosing a yes/no answer to this perpetual question nearly always invites discord and dissension into the family of faith. Instead, treating this as a polarity to be managed not only mirrors the biblical instruction, but generally leads to a more mature and effective leadership culture. Both laity and staff have key roles to play in the leadership of a congregation. Neither can fulfill their calling and potential without the other. Some days the laity lead, some days it is staff, some days it is both, but always it is leadership under the Lordship of Christ.[142]

One can be hard pressed to recognize the Christian ethical dimensions of relationships. For better and worse, pastoral staff and church members have often adapted to their respective cultural context of values as they relate to one another.[143]

We live with the results of centuries of the power distribution in churches being channeled toward the clergy being given (or demanding) the larger portion of power.[144] Even among free church organizations, there remains a tacit hierarchical structure with the pastor and other staff at the top and congregation members at the bottom. This structure is, effectively, little different from the medieval church organization, the polity about which the reformers protested.

For the greater part of the church's history, a great vacuum has occurred with regard to the recapture of the decision making and setting of Christian standards on the part of lay people. For various reasons, too few pastors have taken the initiative to educate membership toward more positive ways of building and securing relationships.

The model suggested here, the priesthood of the believer, is essentially what the reformers like Luther, Calvin, and a host of Anabaptists and Baptists implemented. For them and for the contemporary church, "ministry" is to be the driving force in each life, whether one becomes a medical doctor, plumber, homemaker, information technology expert, pastor, chaplain, and so forth. The ground at the cross is considered level ground.

Some secular organizations reflect a better (more cordial and civil) relational pattern than do churches.

The contemporary prevailing leadership styles move against this level, everyone-is-a-minister model. These contemporary styles promulgate relationships that are uncivil and more reflective of secular organizations than the church. Moreover, some secular organizations reflect a better (more cordial and civil) relational pattern than do churches.

With little or no clergy initiative leading members to take up the ethical reins in their congregation, what has evolved is a subservient, passive, and silent application of Christian ethically shaped relationships by members. As "leadership" is engaged as top-down, or *"whoever is in front* is the leader," little comes from this silent group who ironically are more the church than any single staff member or the whole staff.

The silence has contributed to the decline of the impact of the church in society and in identifying and applying the nature and purpose of the church.[145] The time has more than come when church members must take the initiative, if no one else will, toward building relationships within a congregation that model relational patterns more Christian in substance and style. The informing—and forming—place to begin is where the reformers did, with the New Testament.

A New Testament Perspective

All parties involved in these congregational contexts have abridged, either by ignorance or arrogance, some straightforward guidelines from the New Testament, especially the writings of the Apostle Paul. As Paul corresponded with groups of believers in cities and regions of his time, he said always in the early verses, "To the saints...."

Paul's greeting was inclusive of all who were the followers of Christ, whether leadership types in contemporary categories of pastor or those we would identify as lay people.[146] Following his salutation, Paul gave guidelines for living the Christian life in contextualized ways, with relational accountabilities for all the church—members and leaders.[147]

Paul's guidelines are expressed in various ways, including imperative verbs; conjunctions; eschatological language; the image of putting off and putting on; lists of virtues and vices; calls for character development and especially for being the community of character; ways to think; calls for disciplined speaking; greetings; benedictions; doxologies; and triads as in faith, hope, and love.[148] With these patterns, Paul conveyed to his readers and hearers that the Christian life is not simply about spirituality or abstract thoughts. Rather, living the Christian life is dynamic, engaging and developing relationships in quantifiable ways.

All these patterns infiltrate, inform, and form the tapestry of the more encompassing ideas that are to exhibit the nature, the purpose, and especially the expression of the church: fellowship, proclamation, teaching, and ministry.[149] These character traits, reflective of the character of God in Christ through the power of the Holy Spirit, are to be utilized.

Venues for Implementing Christian Values in Relationships with Staff

Follow-Up to Search Committee's Work

Preparing for a new staff person to join the team can show a congregation how well they are following New Testament guidelines about the character traits for relationships to one another inside the membership, to those outside the membership, and to those who are chosen to lead them in staff roles.

A helpful arrangement can be the formation of a staff persons–congregation relations group, committee, or covenant group. This staff persons–congregation relations group can be part of the process when establishing a search committee. These persons can act as mediating agents between the respective parties.[150] They assist the staff person in getting acquainted with the membership, the programs of the congregation, the committee structures, the financial processes in place, and the community in which the person will serve.

Too often, attention is paid to the newly arriving staff person while his or her family gets ignored. The staff persons–congregation relations group will be sure to respect and involve the person's family in the process of relating to the congregation. This group can assist the family in finding a residence, schools, and/or employment, depending on the needs the particular family presents. The staff persons–congregation relations group should demonstrate hospitality and caring so the family can integrate into the fellowship and community as easily as possible.

Tenure of the Staff Person—Her or His "Ministry Lifetime" in the Congregation

Conventional wisdom opines that the church staff person and congregants are not to engage in friendships. Real life does not work according to this attempt at objectivity, however. People need caring relationships. Undoubtedly, being in relationship is one of the marks of the image of God implanted in us. The message that should be projected from a congregation is that the people who gather in this membership need one another, engage in common causes with one another, and support and encourage one another—all characteristics of friendship. How is it that conventional wisdom has moved from that statement of Jesus, "I do not call you servants any longer...but I have called you friends" (John 15:15, NRSV), to the current context? We should cultivate friendship even more as we mature as Christians.

The message that should be projected from a congregation is that the people who gather in this membership need one another, engage in common causes with one another, and support and encourage one another.

One of the simplest ways to express support is to show up when the respective staff person is acting in her or his role. Too often, for example, lay people have judged a sermon or the preacher on the basis of it being only a projection of that individual. Barbara Brown Taylor commendably points out that

> ...the sermon proves to be a communal act, not the creation of one person but the creation of a body of people for whom and to whom one of them speaks....If the preacher is also their priest and pastor, then the sermon is theirs in another way. The quality of their life together—the memories, conversations, experiences, and hopes they share—is the fabric from which the sermon

is made. The preacher...never gets into the pulpit without them. Whatever else the sermon is about, it is first of all about them, because they are the community in whose midst the preacher stands. In a very real way the preacher would have no voice without them. By calling someone to preach to them and by listening to that person week after week, a congregation gives their minister both the authority to speak and a relationship from which to speak, so that every sermon begins and ends with them.[151]

Such an exercise takes discipline and time to develop. The exercise could be integral, however, to building a collaborative strategy and tactics for the congregation to function as it should. The sermon is only one element in this ongoing collaboration.

Closure—Planning Ahead
Many pastors and other staff arrive at a congregation with thoughts like these in mind: *I will retire from this place; I have found a group with whom I fit;* or *I can truly call this my place of worship and witness.* Even so, the situation could develop so that the minister will leave. The leaving may be of the minister's choice—or not. The pastor may resign or retire.

Of course, pastors are also terminated, by vote or by pressure from church members. These terminations may be necessary but still awkwardly handled.

Our culture educates us in either-or approaches. A both-and approach points toward being as redemptive as possible, even in the worst of circumstances, so that if a person is to be dismissed, any action the church takes toward dismissal should also be marked by redemptive protocols.[152]

One would hope that the congregation who hires a minister also will begin working with the minister toward a covenant statement regarding the beginning, tenure, and even terms of termination of that person's services, however initiated. The transparency needed for such a covenant requires maturity and forethought on everyone's part. The participating parties can even build into the covenant statement a succession plan. What if the minister stays with the congregation until retirement? How will the minister leave? How will a successor be brought in? Would the advice of the current minister be important to that process?

Conclusion

Oh, that contemporary Christians could be labeled by their surrounding culture as Christlike—because the culture sees relationships in the gatherings of these groups that reflect the ethics of Jesus. Demonstrating those relationships indicates that the congregants can not only affirm verbally their love for one another but also provide authentic, day-to-day relationships that demonstrate that their convictions are focused on loving one another.[153]

Review Questions

1. Is a church to be staff-led or lay-led? Why? How?

2. How can a church implement Christian values in the congregation's relationship with the staff?

PART 2:
Quality Staff Administration Essential

Chapter 8

STAFF ADMINISTRATION: FOUNDATION FOR GOOD STAFF RELATIONSHIPS

By Bernard M. Spooner, Ph.D.

Truett Cathy and his brother Ben started a small grill in 1946 that developed into the Chick-fil-A restaurant company.[154] Years later, after Truett's children grew up and were taking control of Chick-fil-A, they shared with their parents the following covenant they planned to use to guide them:

> We covenant to work cooperatively with each other. In the spirit of humility and dependence on one another and to ensure consistence and unity, we will seek the advice of each other in making major decisions. We will pray for each other and trust God to give us the

strength of character needed to fulfill our stewardship responsibilities.[155]

This covenant states the essence of the spirit and commitment needed in church staff relationships. Yet, without a well-thought-out plan of staff administration, this spirit and commitment is hard to achieve.

In the brief introduction to this book, I suggested that good pastor, staff, and congregational relationships depend on servant leadership and good staff administration.

Chapter 2 of this book dealt with servant leadership.[156] We now turn to the subject of staff administration.

Why Does Staff Administration Matter?

Good staff administration ensures fairness and helps everyone to have clear expectations—the pastor, the staff, and the congregation. Early in my ministry, I came to understand that administration was crucial in achieving purpose. "Administration is the task of discovering and clarifying the goals and purpose of the field it serves and moving in a coherent, comprehensive manner toward their realization."[157] When viewed closely, this definition suggests these two basic elements: (1) determining purpose and (2) implementing purpose. The pastor and leaders of any congregation must give careful attention to clarifying and accomplishing the purposes of the church. Once purpose is clear, the next step is to provide implementation of that purpose. Without a clear understanding of purpose or mission, the pastor, staff, and congregation may drift and be ineffective.

Who decides on the purpose of the church? In many respects, the church's purpose was given by Jesus in the Great Commission in Matthew 28:18–20. However, each church must also carry out that purpose or mission in the context of its community. The vision—future picture—of the church addresses both the purpose of the church and its community or region.

For the purpose of this chapter's discussion, staff administration includes the development of a church staff, the application of church policies related to the staff, and the ongoing process of leading and managing the staff. The basic assumption is that the pastor is the general supervisor of the staff, although other people may share by directly supervising or coordinating some personnel. This will depend on the size of the church and its plan of operation. The rest of this chapter will address some basic elements of staff administration.

Basic Elements of Staff Administration

Develop Personnel Policies

Some years ago while serving with Travis Avenue Baptist Church in Fort Worth, Texas, I worked as staff representative with a three-person subcommittee to revise and update church personnel policies. The chair of the group was a longtime employee of the federal government with experience in personnel administration. Another was a unit manager for a leading Fortune 500 company. The third member was a young businessman who owned his own company, had very few employees, and had very limited benefits for employees. To start the meeting with a note of humor, I suggested that the pastor and staff would be pleased with either the government plan or the generous plan of the large corporation. Everyone laughed out loud, but the young businessman assured me that neither plan was even a remote possibility. Although some churches have generous benefits, all churches find it necessary to do the best they can within the resources available. So no single plan will fit all churches.

What does staff administration have to do with staff relations? Staff administration includes not only good personnel policies but also appropriate supervision, open communications among staff members, and clear expectations that are understood by the pastor and other staff members. These elements are essential to successful relationships.

Quality administration helps to ensure all staff members are treated fairly. Well-thought-through personnel policies address issues of fairness and balance for staff members. Personnel policies give the pastor and other staff supervisors guidelines for their work. They also give the congregation's leaders a way to develop a positive climate and to maintain an effective staff, which helps to ensure healthy church relationships.

Choose an informed, qualified team to review or develop policies. A qualified group of respected church leaders is needed for such an important task. It is wise to place at least one person on the committee who has experience with business or institution personnel matters. It is especially important to have people on the group who have good attitudes toward the pastor and staff and who understand and have the confidence of the congregation. It is also wise to have the pastor or a nonvoting staff representative serving with this group.

Good personnel policies can be both caring and based on sound business practices. They should protect both church personnel and the church.

The approach of the Fort Worth church team was to review and update the written policies already in place. For a church with no formal written policies, a good way to start is to write down the practices already being used. Furthermore, the committee members may develop a list of questions they feel the policies need to answer. For example, what do we do when a staff member has a serious or extended illness or has a death in the family? How much vacation do the pastor and other staff members get each year? How do we determine the salaries for our ministers and support personnel? What is our plan for calling a pastor? How do we go about a search and call for other ministers? How do we employ support staff such as ministry assistants, food service personnel, and custodians?

Write personnel policies. The following steps are suggested:

- *Secure copies of the church's current written policies, if available.* Otherwise, write up the practices being used by the pastor, staff supervisors, and personnel committee. Most churches have some ongoing practices they use as they employ staff.

- *Secure and review policies from other churches of similar size and resources in the general geographical region.* The workgroup may also check church websites to find policies. This step provides new ideas about how to approach various policies or benefits. (Appendix I may be useful for this purpose.)
- *Review current policies and consider updating areas that may have been changed by church action or by some recent development.* For example, the pastor or the personnel committee may be using some practices that have not been formally approved.
- *Before finalizing the new policies, seek input.* For example, it would be wise to share them with the pastor and other staff supervisors. Also, the full personnel committee should have an opportunity to give input before policies move through the church approval process.
- *Once the above steps have been taken, the final step is to get the policies officially approved by the church.* Generally, it is best to have the congregation approve the policies since there are legal aspects to personnel matters.

Develop position descriptions. Why have job descriptions? They serve as a basis for understanding the work of each person on the staff. They provide staff members clear work assignments. It is important to group common tasks together to avoid overlapping of duties. Furthermore, when communicated to the congregation, members know whom to go to for help they need. A job description is the starting point for good delegation of work.

A good way to start preparing job descriptions is to have current staff members write down the tasks they do. Some may have been given a job description when they were first employed. As time has passed, some tasks may have been added or dropped, but it is good to find out from all personnel what they are currently doing.

Another good practice is to study job descriptions from other churches. Some excellent job descriptions are provided in Appendix I. Churches take different approaches for organizing the work of staff members and in the way tasks are assigned, but reviewing job descriptions of other churches may prove to be useful.

It is also helpful to develop a common format for all job descriptions such as the one for minister of education, provided in this chapter. This job description is also shown in Appendix I.

Minister of Education
First Baptist Church, Garland, Texas

Summary: To provide leadership for the development, coordination, and effectiveness of the overall Christian education ministries of the church.

Reports To: Senior Pastor.

Minimum Qualifications: Christian education (CE) related seminary (master's degree preferred) and at least seven years of effective local church experience in a similar ministry role within church(es) with similar ministry philosophy, structure, and direction as First Baptist Garland.

Duties/Responsibilities

- Coordinate the work of the education staff team (ministers, directors, and support staff).
    - o Help set the vision, purpose, and direction of the overall CE ministry.
    - o Work with education staff to interpret this vision/ purpose/direction for each age division.
    - o Coach the education staff in providing effective leadership to their teams of paid and volunteer leaders.

- o Provide consistent communication regarding progress and issues related to each age division.
- o Ensure needs for space, equipment, and resources are sufficiently anticipated, planned for, and met for all age divisions. (This includes coordination with other staff outside the Education Staff Team.)

- Give specific direction to the adult education ministries of the church.
  - o Recruit, train, and encourage leaders in the Sunday School/Open Group ministries, discipleship ministries, and any other Christian education ministries for adults.
  - o Ensure curriculum, supplies, and resources are provided.
  - o Communicate vision/purpose/direction (noted above) with applicable adult CE leaders.

- Serve as staff liaison for men's ministry leadership
  - o Be available to provide support and consultation to volunteer leaders in this area regarding planning and coordination of their ministry efforts.
  - o Provide input on the CE-related functions of this ministry.

- Give direction for the church's overall outreach/evangelism ministry efforts.
  - o Evaluate and implement improvements as necessary.
  - o Ensure the Great Commission mandate is being maintained as a key ingredient of all ministries in some form.
  - o Model, encourage, and equip others to be a witness in their personal circles of contact and influence.

- Implement and oversee the church's assimilation process for new church members.
- Maintain professional awareness and expertise in the field of Christian Education.
- Other duties assigned by supervisor.

Note that this job description specifies the position title, the supervisor, minimum qualifications, and duties and responsibilities, with necessary details under each major assignment. Individual churches will choose formats that meet their needs. The Austin Baptist Church in Austin, Texas, has a similar format but also includes a section, "Evaluation and Compensation," which states that the position will receive a performance evaluation and compensation, reviewed annually.

Determine What Staff Will Be Needed for the Future

The pastor of a large church called me one day and asked me to come to his church and help figure out what staff they would need for the next twenty years. I asked, "What kind of ministry does your church plan to do over the next twenty years?" I helped him see that the staff needed would depend on the vision he and the congregation would be addressing. A congregation must provide the appropriate resources for the mission and vision for their field of ministry—locally and worldwide. Over the years I have helped a number of churches think through their staff plan. It always bothers me to think of staff personnel as a resource. However, the budget, facilities, the pastor and staff, and the members of the congregation are all parts of God's resources for impacting the community. The following steps can be followed to determine appropriate staffing:

1. *Begin by setting up a special committee or team to formally address the question.* It may be best to use a special study group as the process will require looking at all church ministries and the church community. The group should be

representative of the congregation and include persons from all age groups and ministries. It should include men and women familiar with all aspects of church life. Also, the pastor and key leadership staff should be involved. A good study will take three to six months.

2. *Gather church statistics for the last five to ten years.* This information will inform the workgroup about how the church is changing. Statistics should include baptisms, Sunday School and/or small group ministries, missions, music ministries, and other programs. Also, financial information should be included along with the history of church staff additions or changes.

3. *Provide demographic information for the community and surrounding areas.* Census data should include population changes and information about the various people groups in the community, their educational and income levels, housing trends, and so on. Often, church members and some staff will be surprised at the changes taking place. Local school boards, city officials, or your local or state denominational offices will be good sources for demographic data.

4. *Think forward about a vision or "future picture" for your community and your congregation.* Ask, "What changes in our community offer opportunities both in the near term and for several years ahead? How can addressing some of these changes make our church more effective in reaching persons in our community?" As these questions are being addressed by the committee, it may be helpful to do a congregational survey to develop broad input for use by the committee. When the final report is presented, the congregation also should receive a summary of the information developed by the study committee.

5. *Develop some priorities for the future and set goals that focus on each priority.* The committee should limit the priorities to only three or four areas of opportunity and set only one or two goals for each priority. The priorities and goals should address church and community findings and input from the congregation. Some goals such as building a new building may take a decade or more to accomplish; however, most goals should be for only one, two, or three years into the future. It should be understood that goals will be adjusted as experience and changing circumstances suggest. All goals should be achievable, measurable, have a target date for completion, and be assigned to an individual or group for action.

6. *Propose recommendations for the personnel committee and the congregation.* It is now time to consider staff needs for the future. After going through the five steps listed, the committee now has the information needed to help determine what staff is needed for the future. One question to be answered is, "What staff will be needed to implement the proposed priorities and goals of the church?" Others are, "Can our current staff be reorganized to lead the congregation in addressing the priorities and to achieve the goals? If new staff is needed, what kind of education/training and experience will they need to be effective?" Another good question is, "Can this ministry be done through current lay leadership?"

7. *Prepare the staff and congregation for any changes proposed.* Good communication is essential to good relationships, and changes need to be carefully and thoughtfully communicated. Some staff members may need to take on additional assignments, and others may take part of the assignment of another staff member or have a part of their assignment given to a proposed new staff member. All change, whether for

ministry staff or support personnel, requires adjustments by the staff and by the congregation.

8. *Develop a table of organization.* This table of organization will help communicate how staff members relate to one another, and it will help the congregation understand how the plan works. Communicating the table of organization and staff job descriptions to the congregation ensures that everyone will know to whom to go for help.

Develop a Staff Salary Plan

Why is a staff salary plan important? A well-thought-through staff salary plan can help in many ways. It will ensure fairness for all staff members. It can help to maximize the financial resources available for staff personnel. It will help in determining whether the congregation can afford to add additional staff.

Leaders need to be very careful to approve new staff only after they ensure the church budget can support current employees. Although the staff is crucial to the ministry of a church, the personnel budget must be kept in balance with the total ministry of the church. Keeping a good balance not only protects those already employed but also helps to ensure that other church needs are met. Missions, ongoing local ministries, and facility maintenance and development are essential for a church as it carries out its New Testament mandates. Therefore, all church needs should be kept in clear focus along with personnel costs.

Use a good process for developing a salary plan. Begin by asking some questions, such as: "How valuable is each position to the basic mission and vision of the congregation? How broad is the influence of this position to the church as a whole? Is this position essential to the effectiveness of the church? What level of education and experience is needed for each position? What is the degree of difficulty of this position compared to all other positions?" Generally, the pastor's role is considered to be the most difficult and of the greatest value to the overall welfare of the church, and so this position may be weighted highest. On the other hand, although the work of a custodian is important, it may be rated as the lowest in the degree of difficulty and value to the congregation. Staff members who lead a broad range of ministries and significantly impact the church's effectiveness would rate high in the degree of difficulty, impact, and overall influence, while the rest would rate up and down through the scale.

For example, a staff member who supervises several age group ministers and is responsible for much of the administration may be rated very high on the scale. The minister responsible for leading worship and an all-age music ministry would rate high on the scale. Of course, all positions should contribute to the church and be essential. The staff work group should rate all positions from the pastor to the custodian and establish a salary range for each position. It is helpful to have beginning, middle, and maximum salaries for each position. This process provides a way to think through all salaries to ensure each staff member is being fairly compensated for the tasks required.[158]

The following steps can be used to rank staff positions:

1. Hand out a set of updated job descriptions to each member of the workgroup.

2. Without discussion, ask each committee member to rate all job descriptions based on the skills and abilities required to do the job. For example, if there are seven (7) positions, they are to rank the job requiring the greatest skills, abilities, and education as 1. The position requiring the least skills is rated 7, or last. All positions are to be given a rank based on the individual study of the job descriptions.

3. Without discussion, the chairperson has each person report his or her ratings while the chairperson records them on a

marker board or chart. The chair then averages the rankings given for each job by all committee members.

4. The committee is now ready to discuss the results of this process. Each member should give his or her general impression of the results and raise points of disagreement. The discussion continues until consensus is reached. Some positions may be determined to have the same ranking, even if the job descriptions are different.

These steps can be used to determine a salary scale:

1. If practical, make a survey of salaries of similar positions in other local churches in your community or in nearby locations. Care should be taken to be sure the job descriptions are comparable. One issue I experienced more than once in determining salaries of age group ministers was a committee's comparison to public school teachers. Certainly, this is a good reference point; however, most age group ministers function more like assistant principals who have administrative and leadership responsibilities. They must enlist, train, and lead a corps of workers. Also, they must motivate and supervise their workers. That being said, many churches may not be able even to pay salaries equal to that of local schoolteachers.

2. Determine the minimum and maximum salary for each position based on the rankings and the survey data. It is recommended that a percentage method be used for arriving at minimums and maximum salaries. Leonard Wedel[159] suggests a 35 percent range from the minimum to the maximum for each position. See the example below. Of course, the beginning salary for a newly employed person would be somewhere in between the top and bottom figure, depending

on the individual's experience and the church's financial strength.

Salary Rating	Beginning	Mid-Point	Maximum
Number 1	$80,000	$94,000	$108,000
Number 2	$65,000	$76,375	$87,750
Number 3	$55,000	$64,625	$74,250
Number 4	$45,000	$52,875	$60,750
Number 10	$26,000	$30,550	$35,100

3. Once a salary plan is established, it may take several years to be fully implemented. It is not essential for every change to be established at once. Good staff relationships call for caution and sensitivity on the part of the pastor, the personnel committee, and staff supervisors. As new staff members are employed, the plan should be used as fully as practical. For example, as salaries are reviewed each year, some adjustments can be made to move toward the plan.

Implement a Process for Staff Appraisal and Development

Over the years, I have been exposed to a number of approaches for staff appraisal. When first exposed to annual appraisals, I was uncomfortable with it. However, I came to see the appraisal process as *staff member development and planning* and became comfortable with it. I came to see the supervisor's role as one of guiding and developing those they supervise and lead.

My very first experience with staff appraisal and development was interesting, to say the least. The plan called for me to do the appraisal with my supervisor observing. The employee filled out his own appraisal of himself, and I also filled out my appraisal of the employee. He was a longtime employee whom I had known for many years. Furthermore, my boss's daughter had married this employee's son, which added another dimension to the event. When I started the appraisal, my boss observing, I discovered the employee had marked himself with the very highest rating on every point of the appraisal chart. This made for an interesting discussion. I decided to assure him that all of us can continue to improve in effectiveness, and we both agreed to lower those scores to a more realistic level. After the meeting, my supervisor commended me for the way I handled the situation.

Why bother with such a process? How does an employee know what is "really" expected? There must be quality communication from the beginning. The appraisal interview is not the time to reveal a list of discrepancies. These should have been discussed along the way as such issues were observed. The appraisal interview is a time to look at the big picture and to think ahead. At the same time, it is important to deal with specific problems in a more general way. Although a leader may need to discuss a problem with a staff member, this should be done as quickly as is possible and appropriate after the problem occurs. The discussion should be done privately and not in front of others, such as in staff meetings. The appraisal visit provides an extended time to review expectations, to set benchmarks for ministry, and to help staff members think longer-range.

Often new staff members are given a good welcome as they begin their work. They attend staff meetings and ask questions as needed to do their regular day-to-day tasks. In fact, most staff members do what they understand their jobs to be. As time goes by, the supervisor may see some weaknesses in the effectiveness of a staff member, or some church members may report disappointment over some action or approach taken by the staff member. A good supervisor will take time to help the staff member immediately upon seeing such a problem arise.

To help staff members develop a broad vision for their area of ministry, annual or semiannual formal conversations are essential. This is a time to review progress, think ahead, and plan for personal development. Often, through this process, a new level of effectiveness may be achieved. This process can give employees increased confidence and help them find greater fulfillment in their work. It may also help them to be better team members.

Where does the process start? A goal-setting and review process is central to day-to-day supervision. To understand the role of this process, it is necessary to first understand the planning process.

Within the context of church priorities and goals, personnel should be asked to develop annual plans and goals related to their job description assignments. The plan should define specific individual goals for the coming year, identify plans for achieving the goals, and set estimated completion dates for each goal. Note: These goals and plans should include the expectation for developing and maintaining good relationships with other employees and church members.

Goals provide the cornerstone on which supervisors and employees organize their work and integrate their effort. Performance planning and review is the process that provides focus to each employee's role in contributing to the accomplishment of these goals.

What are some key steps in the process? The process itself consists of a number of sequential steps:

(1) When the staff member is hired, the supervisor discusses the purpose and major responsibilities of his or her job. This is done by reviewing together the formal job description for the position. Also, the supervisor shares the current vision for the church, the church priorities, and church goals.

(2) The supervisor identifies key areas where the employee can contribute to the church priorities and goals. In turn, the staff member is asked to set his or her own measureable goals for addressing both the churchwide goals and the goals for his or her specific ministry area. Each goal should have a target date for achievement. Most goals will be for a year or less; however, some may extend beyond one year.

(3) Once the employee sets his or her goals, the next step is to develop action plans for each goal. Goals will be accomplished by taking action. The supervisor may need to brainstorm

with the employee to come up with ideas for action plans. Also, some employees may feel it necessary to discuss some action plans with volunteer leaders.

(4) Supervisors and employees should have brief checkup meetings from time to time to review progress toward goals or to modify plans and goals where necessary. For new employees, it is advisable to hold the goal-setting meeting during their first or second month on the job.

(5) At the end of the year, the supervisor and the employee review the employee's accomplishments. This review is a time to provide important input for setting new goals, and the cycle begins anew.

The worksheets that follow may be helpful as a planning tool. The first sheet, "Beginning of the Year," may be used for planning at the beginning of the cycle. Some leaders may want to include signature lines and dates for the meeting at the beginning of the year and for the review meeting at the end of the cycle.

Beginning of the Year: Goals and Action Plan Worksheet

Goals and Action Steps	Priority by Percent	Completion Date
Goal 1: Improve the level of outreach and caring ministry within each teaching group	30%	**October 15**

- *Action 1*: Conduct an input meeting with department directors and teachers to get ideas.
- *Action 2*: Schedule two training sessions in how to reach and care for persons related to this age group.
- *Action 3*: Schedule three major outreach activities during the year designed to reach persons of this age group.

Goal 2: Recruit, train and deploy 10 new teachers	30%	**January 1**

- **Action 1**: Ask current directors, workers, and adult teachers for suggestions for new teachers.
- **Action 2**: Schedule and prepare a training course for potential teachers.
- **Action 3**. Work with directors to enlist potential teachers to attend the training class.
- **Action 4**. Conduct the training course and help participants to determine where they will serve.

Goal 3: Improve the level of ministry to families related to groups in this age group	30%	**August 1**

- **Action 1**: Conduct an input meeting with department directors and teachers to get ideas.
- **Action 2**: Schedule visits into each home related to this age group.
- **Action 3**: Schedule two family fellowship events to include children and their families including grandparents.

Goal 4: Improve the attractiveness of our facilities	10%	**August 1**

- **Action 1**: Conduct an input meeting with department directors and teachers to get ideas.
- **Action 2**: Schedule at least one Saturday morning in the early spring as a "First Impressions Day."
- **Action 3**: Invite parents and grandparents to participate.

The following sheet, "End of the Year," may be used at the end of the cycle as a review of the results. Some goals might not have been achieved; nonetheless, this is not a time for the supervisor to criticize the staff member. Rather, it is a time for the employee to see the results of his or her planning and to think ahead to the next year of ministry. Very likely, the supervisor will already know how well the plans have been achieved and will be ready to give encouragement as the next year begins. As mentioned previously, part of the second meeting should be used to review goals for the coming year. Of course, new goals will arise as new needs are discovered and as the priorities of the church have developed.

End of the Year: Goals and Action Plans Review Worksheet

Goals	Priority by Percent	Completion Date
Goal 1: Improve the level of outreach and caring ministry within each teaching group	30%	October 15
Goal 2: Recruit, train and deploy 10 new teachers	30%	January 1
Goal 3: Improve the level of ministry to families related to groups in this age group	30%	August 1
Goal 4: Improve the attractiveness of our facilities	10%	August 1

Enrich and Develop Staff Members

The pastor and all staff members need to continue to learn and grow as individuals as they serve their congregation. This is good for both the leadership and the congregation. A growing staff member will feel he or she is progressing in ministry, and the congregation will benefit as well. Most churches encourage staff members to attend conferences or seminars related to their vocational role in the church. For example, an age group minister should be encouraged to attend conferences provided by the denomination or by professional associations. Of course, the church will need to budget funds for this purpose. Also, planning to participate in these events should become a part of the appraisal and development process.

Many churches provide resources to assist staff members with opportunities to upgrade their knowledge and skills related to assigned responsibilities. Some staff members are allowed to enroll in an advanced degree program related to their assignment. Completing the degree may require several years, with the staff member being gone for one or two days several times a year. Yet, as the person does this study, the church immediately gains as the staff member begins to implement the new ideas and insights being learned. I was fortunate that the Travis Avenue Baptist Church in Fort Worth allowed me to pursue a doctorate after I had been on the staff for a few years. When the time came for me to finalize my dissertation, I was allowed to be relieved of most duties for six weeks.

It is becoming more common today to see churches give brief sabbaticals to pastors and sometimes other staff members, especially after they have served for an extended time at the church. These opportunities may require a supply preacher or for someone else to assume some of the staff member's duties while the staff member is away. Staff members must be sensitive to the needs of the church when such opportunities are offered. The timing should never result in the church being neglected. Hence, great care should be taken to ensure that appropriate arrangements are made for church ministries to continue as fully as possible.

Conclusion

We should understand that all people, including church staff, will have issues that cause conflict and misunderstanding. At the same time, it is important for every person to feel included and to be affirmed in his or her role on the church staff and among church members. Perhaps we should pledge to each other, as the Chick-fil-A family does:

> We covenant to work cooperatively with each other. In the spirit of humility and dependence on one another and to ensure consistence and unity, we will seek the advice of each other in making major decisions. We will pray for each other and trust God to give us the strength of character needed to fulfill our stewardship responsibilities.[160]

Review Questions

1. Why does church staff administration matter?

2. What are some basic elements of church staff administration?

3. How would you begin to enhance or develop and implement a plan for church staff administration?

Suggestions for Further Reading

R.K. Greenleaf. *The Servant as Leader.* Westfield, IN: The Greenleaf Center for Servant Leadership, 1970.

Alvin G. Lindgren. *Foundations for Purposeful Church Administration.* Nashville, TN: Abingdon Press, 1965.

Peter G. Northouse. *Leadership Theory and Practice.* Sixth edition. Los Angeles, London, New Delhi, Singapore, and Washington DC: Sage, 2013.

Bruce P. Powers. *Church Administration Handbook.* Nashville, TN: Broadman and Holman Press, 1997.

Charles A. Tidwell. *Church Administration: Effective Leadership for Ministry.* Nashville, TN: Broadman Press, 1985.

Leonard E. Wedel. *Building and Maintaining a Church Staff.* Nashville, TN: Broadman Press, 1966.

Robert H. Welch. *Church Administration: Creating Efficiency for Effective Ministry.* Nashville, TN: Broadman and Holman Press, 2011.

Chapter 9

PLANNING WITH STAFF AND CONGREGATIONAL LEADERSHIP: DYNAMIC PLANNING RELATIONSHIPS

By Morlee Maynard, D.Ed.Min.

How often do we hear the following complaints? "Our people won't do anything!" "The most we have serving in some way is 20 percent of our people." "People are indifferent when thinking about serving God." The list could go on, but let's stop ignoring the realities behind these complaints. Could we make the assumption that many adult church members are serving God in a variety of ways in their homes, workplaces, and neighborhoods? LifeWay Research discovered through their Transformational Discipleship Assessment instrument, that when asked to respond to the statement: "I intentionally try to serve people outside my church who have tangible needs," 60 percent agreed, although only 17 percent strongly agreed. Fifteen percent of those surveyed disagreed with the statement.[161] They were just not serving *at* their churches the way church leaders want them to when they need to fill teaching positions and other ongoing ministries.

Peter Marshall (1902–1949), the author, preacher, and chaplain of the United States Senate, made a remarkable observation: "A different world cannot be made by indifferent people."[162] Perhaps the same could be said about men and women regarding their attitudes and perceptions about their churches. Often, church polity and practices limit the number of people who *get to* actively participate in decision making and planning. Conversely, an understanding of what makes Boomers, Busters, and Millennials tick points the way to move them from indifference to passion—by engaging them at some level in church decision making and planning processes. James Estep called for churches to engage people from a high value of humanity "because we are the *imageo dei*, the image of God... (Gen. 1:27)."[163] In unique ways, adults want to participate in creating their own activities, including the ways they carry out God's calling on their lives to use their spiritual gifts to glorify him.

Moving adults from the status quo to passion through a planning process calls for churches to have some sort of planning system that is set in the context of relationships. In his book *Church Administration*, Robert Welch defined planning as a task that visualizes the mission of the church to see the church moving in the future. He clarified planning as "the work we do to predetermine a course of action. Planning is concerned with the futurity of present decisions—that is, what will happen in the future with the decisions we make now."[164] Notice the word "we." Who does the visualizing? To get enthusiastic support and ownership of the direction a church family is moving, everyone needs the opportunity to participate at some level in visualizing the future and planning how *we* will get there. Estep says, "The spiritual and familiar relationship we share as Christians must underlie, and on occasion supersede, the institutional necessities of relationship within the Christian institution."[165] Only God knows the future, but through a relational planning process, pastors and leadership teams have the opportunity to capture the imaginations and desires of their church families connecting to God's guidance to the future.

Moving adults from the status quo to passion through a planning process calls for churches to have some sort of planning system that is set in the context of relationships.

The way to capture the imaginations and desires of church families takes place in the context of collaborative relationships. In his book, *Church Unique*, Will Mancini introduced coordination and collaboration as strategic stages to align all ministries to the church's vision and mission. "Collaboration is the point where individual ministries and leaders have checked their ego at the door and are actively trying to serve the mission by serving one another."[166] When egos are out of the way, relationships are forged in Christ's love. Consequently, collaboration sets the stage for productive idea-sharing and cooperation.

The purpose of this chapter is to encourage and inspire church leaders to coordinate and collaborate (plan) with church members through a set of actions (strategy) to accomplish the mission and vision. In order to explore the concept of dynamic planning relationships, let's ask the following questions: Why plan in the context of relationships? What does relational planning look like? How does planning through cooperation and collaboration work?

Why Plan in the Context of Relationships?

The Great Commission (Matthew 28:18–20) is often used to foster a church culture that cares more about people who are not members of the church than those who are members. For example,

Sunday School teachers are often encouraged to leave one chair empty to remind everyone to invite those who are not participating in their groups. Bob Mayfield, Sunday School director for the Baptist General Convention of Oklahoma, encourages Sunday School teachers to put a page on the bulletin board for members to write the first names of their friends who need Jesus Christ and a church family. In his book, *Missional Renaissance*, Reggie McNeal identified such practices to be part of a missional movement. This movement involves three shifts in how churches think and carry out ministry: from internal to external ministry focus, from program development to people development activities, and from church-based to kingdom-based agenda.[167]

A church that has a missional culture depends on a comprehensive planning system that dynamically involves everyone in accomplishing the vision, focusing on making disciples, thinking strategically, establishing priorities, and sequencing activities for accomplishing their goals. Consider these reasons to use a dynamic planning system in the context of relationships.

First, why would the majority of church members support and participate in a missional attitude without being involved in planning how their churches will carry out the Great Commission? For a church to serve from a missional standpoint, each individual member needs to live his or her life from a missional perspective. McNeal referred to such a perspective as treating life relationships[168] as kingdom opportunities. The opportunity to participate will encourage members to be aware of people around them who need the Lord. Such awareness leads to action.

Second, why would church members be willing to accept the church's decision to end ministries that do not focus on making disciples? When they are given the opportunity to participate in simplifying all that a church family does, they have the opportunity to understand and accept the needed ministry cuts. In his book *Simple Church*, Eric Geiger championed the need to align everything a church does to a simple-to-understand disciple-making process.[169] The relationships play a major role in strengthening how churches engage the needed changes that will enable them to accomplish their visions for making disciples for Jesus Christ.

Third, why would church members go along with these changes without seeing an intentional strategy that will take the church in the right direction for accomplishing their vision? The best way to get the support and buy-in from church members is to give them the opportunity to participate in an intentional way as the strategy is being developed.

Fourth, why would church members support missional actions if these actions are not derived from the core values of the church? According to Audrey Malphurs, core values dictate personal involvement in the ministries of a church.[170] The priorities of a church family are based on their stated and real core values. More church members will get excited about missional thinking when the various actions directly relate to the corporate core values of the church. Again, the opportunity to participate in the identification of priorities based on core values will enable church members to support and get excited about carrying out actions that launch efforts to reach those who do not know Jesus as their Savior.

And fifth, why would church members take the time to participate in missional efforts if they have not had some say in the sequencing of the actions to reach beyond the walls of the church building? People are busy. Families are busy. When church members are given the opportunity to participate in developing these missional actions, smarter decisions will be made about timing and scheduling. Welch put this conversation in simple terms, "programming is setting up a sequence of events that will lead to objective completion."[171] Programming speaks to actions taken to reach goals. Planning is the process for determining the actions to take going forward.

All five of these reasons for involving people in a dynamic planning process build a strong case for coordination and collaboration. Involving people in planning is giving God the opportunity to empower God's people to deepen relationships with himself, among themselves, and with those beyond the walls.

What Does Relational Planning Look Like?

Perhaps the practice of intentionally giving God the opportunity to empower God's people by involving all church members in planning processes is culturally impossible for many churches. The pastor and deacons have always done it. Or the church leadership team (church council) handles it for everyone else. British Baptist pastor Charles Spurgeon (1834–1892) believed that "planning was important but that one must always recognize God's sovereign leading in any plans that one makes in this life. 'In his heart a man plans his course, but the LORD determines his steps' (Prov. 16:9 NIV). Once we know God's plan for us, we are then free to pursue God's plan for action as we seek to accomplish his purpose."[172] When church leaders have some sense of God's plan for individual members, they are better able to pursue God's plan for the church as a whole.

When church leaders have some sense of God's plan for individual members, they are better able to pursue God's plan for the church as a whole.

Let's consider various ways to involve everyone in the planning process. All church members participate in the planning process through their small groups (Sunday School, home groups, or whatever small group organization is used by a church). Many of the church members who serve on committees or teams will also participate in the planning processes set up for committees and teams. And the vocational ministers who make up the church staff will also participate in planning processes designed for their ministries.

Small Groups

One major cultural change would set the stage for God to empower everyone, not just a few. Jesus told his disciples "I assure you: The one who believes in Me will also do the works that I do. And he will do even greater works than these, because I am going to the Father" (John 14:12, HCSB).[173] When Jesus appeared to his disciples after his crucifixion, he commissioned them, "Peace to you, As the Father has sent Me, I also send you" (John 20:21, HCSB). George Cladis summarized this context when he wrote, "Each member of the body has a unique role to play and is gifted by God to do it. We are interconnected in a network of relationships with Christ as the head.[174] Consequently, the culture of churches is enhanced by accepting the fact that God wants everyone, not just those who serve as vocational ministers, to serve and glorify him.

Many Bible study groups are engaging this fact—that all believers are ministers—by considering their experiences in group Bible study on Sunday mornings, Wednesday evenings, or during a weekday as a time for member ministers to meet and grapple with the application of the Bible study to their ministries. They start by sharing what God did through them the previous week. As they read and examine the Scriptures, they draw direct implications of what God is teaching them through the verses to impact their ministries. They conclude each Bible study by reflecting on what God wants them to do in light of these verses. These small groups become accountability groups for their members.

A strategic way to hold each other accountable is to involve the small groups in the church planning process. Through these small groups of ministers, churches are multiplying intentional missional actions that cause church members to look for what God wants them to be and do where they work and live. As a church launches its annual planning process, small group leaders are trained in how to engage group members in prayerfully planning their ministries for the next year.

The basic question is, "What does God want me to do this year at home, at work, at church, in the community, and in the world?"

Many churches have a questionnaire for committee and team leaders to use as a guide in making their plans for the year. The same or a similar form could be used by small group leaders with their group members. The purpose of the form is to get people to think about their actions to spiritually grow and serve God in the coming year. The basic question is, "What does God want me to do this year at home, at work, at church, in the community, and in the world?" The form causes them to consider ministry actions, such as to develop a relationship with a colleague who does not know Jesus, serve on a teaching team with one of the age group ministries in the church, sponsor a neighborhood Bible study for a few weeks during the year, and take action on a ministry passion that God keeps nudging them to do. The form might also ask them to plan actions to grow spiritually during the year such as to identify biblical topics of interest for study or to develop a relationship with a spiritual coach. Families could also fill out the form as a way to challenge family members to talk about how they will serve the Lord and grow spiritually as a family.

The small group leaders need a way to collect the forms to turn in to the church office. The forms could be filled out either anonymously or with names. Each member needs to keep a copy of his or her form to follow during the year. The small group leaders may also want a copy of the completed forms for their groups to use in planning what God wants to do through them as a group in the coming year.

When all the members know that the church plans will be based on their personal plans, the members will have a sense of ownership of the plans the church leaders will be presenting at a later time.

The church staff or leadership team can use the member ministry plans as the basis for making the church plans for the year. When all the members know that the church plans will be based on their personal plans, the members will have a sense of ownership of the plans the church leaders will be presenting at a later time. This participation shows members that they are respected and accepted as integral participants in the church planning process, a key to relationships.

Leadership Communities

All churches have a variety of leadership communities. In addition to the small group Bible study ministry teams, churchwide ministry teams handle all the actions to involve the church family in Bible study, fellowship, discipleship, worship, and ministry. These teams include the deacons, the Lord's Supper ministry team, missions team, fellowship team, and others. Committees carry out decisions regarding administrative concerns such as the finances, personnel, and property. Many churches have a community of all the leaders of the committees and teams, such as the church council or church leadership community.

A variety of planning processes are used by churches. One process used by many churches asks the committees and teams to fill out *MAPP* (Ministry · Action · Purpose · Plans) forms for the coming year. The committee and team leaders are encouraged to involve the members of their team members in planning what to put on their *MAPPs*. The *MAPP* form includes the church's mission statement and the vision that drives what the teams and committees do with their plans and actions. The *MAPPs* are turned in and compiled into a church planning grid. As plans are formalized, the committee and team leaders meet to coordinate their ideas with the pastor and church staff and collaborate through some sort of meeting, perhaps an annual meeting.

This annual meeting enables the committee and team leaders to meet with each other. They have a meal together and enjoy a time of fellowship. They also meet quarterly through the year to intentionally celebrate, review, and touch base on how their plans are taking place. The *MAPPs* serve as the connections for enhancing relationships among the leaders.

Church Staff (Vocational Ministers)

For most churches, the pastor and staff cause the coordination and collaboration to take place. The relational aspect of the planning strategy is contingent on the attitudes and modeling for coordination and collaboration done by the pastor and staff. When the pastor and church staff members relate to one another in a collegial way, the member ministers will have the opportunity to learn how to do the same with the staff as well as among themselves.

A relational planning process that involves all church members gives the vocational ministers a great tool for doing their part in the planning process. For example, youth ministers work through the *MAPP* with their teachers or department directors. The worship ministers use the *MAPP* process with their choir leaders or worship teams.

Remember those forms completed by member ministers in the small groups? Those forms can be a variation of the *MAPP* form. For example, when collected by the staff members who plan adult Bible studies during the year, they can easily be used to determine what to offer during the coming year. The staff members who organize mission trips can easily learn where people are being called to go on mission. Age group ministers who staff various teaching ministries each year have a way to evaluate how effective their processes are for involving people in their ministries. The church staff will find a variety of ways to incorporate the member *MAPPs* into their church ministry *MAPPs*. Member ministers will then see their churches responding to their passions and interests in ways that launch them into ministry and spiritual growth.

How Does Planning Through Coordination and Collaboration Work?

With the information gleaned from the member minister, committee, and ministry team *MAPPs*, the ministerial staff members collaborate to develop their plans for the coming year. This collaboration takes place during special gatherings such as retreats and weekly staff meetings. These gatherings need to be planned carefully by the facilitators. Without such planning, time is often wasted, and relationships are compromised. All three types of planning comprise the planning strategy—framing the vision (sometimes called strategic planning), annual planning (resulting in the annual budget), and ongoing planning.

Framing the Vision

For years, churches have done strategic planning. Many churches have followed the steps provided by Aubrey Malphurs in his book *Advanced Strategic Planning: A New Model for Church and Ministry Leaders,* second edition. These steps include discovering core values, developing a mission, creating a vision, identifying actions to accomplish the vision, implementing the plan, and evaluation. Many churches use this process to plan the next three to five years.

Reggie McNeal contributed to the planning movement through his book *The Present Future: Six Tough Questions for the Church* by calling for strategic *thinking* instead of strategic *planning.*[175] Strategic thinking enables churches to think in terms of preparing for the challenges ahead.

In recent years, a new generation has stepped off of Malphurs's process to develop a process that focuses the church on the vision for the future. Will Mancini is a leader in this movement. He explained his process in his book, *Church Unique: How Missional Leaders Cast Vision, Capture Culture, and Create Movement*. His process is called "Vision Framework." As churches become more and more missional in their visions for the future, planning strategies will change and become more customized to the culture of each individual church.

Whatever process a church develops for planning actions to accomplish their vision, the relational aspects will become more and more important as younger generations move in to leadership positions. The changing cultures of churches will influence where and how the church gathers to work through the process. Some churches will host spiritual retreats for members to consider what they want to do in the next period of time to prepare themselves to face the challenges of living in an increasingly post-Christian world. Churches will have leadership retreats for the pastor and staff to compile the interests, needs, and desires of the church members as expressed on their personal plans. Based on this information, they will develop the vision framework or strategic plan. These retreats will launch the planning process, which will be followed up by ongoing gatherings to craft a set of actions for the next period of time.

Annual Planning

With the vision framework or strategic plan in hand, the pastor, staff members, and leadership community (committee and team leaders) can consider what they will do during the coming year. To implement the big picture, they should consider what will be accomplished each year. Goal setting is a collaborative way of beginning such annual planning. In the book *Management Essentials for Christian Ministries*, Gary Bredfelt states that "effective leadership demands the development of goal-setting skills. Leaders must be able to guide ministry team members in establishing team goals and in forming and reaching personal goals."[176] He goes on to delineate the contributions of group goals and personal goals to the overall planning process: "Group goals give ministry efforts direction toward a unified mission. Personal goals foster motivation, a sense of achievement, and a means of improvement for each team participant."[177] He suggests that church leaders take the time to involve members in the goal setting process. By using the *MAPPs* process, the goals can be derived from the "plans" section of member ministers, committee, and teams *MAPPs*. Bredfelt also suggests a member input process that uses a survey form that identifies the proposed church goals.[178] The plans and goals on the *MAPPs* may become valuable tools in tracking progress in each of the ministries. Whatever steps church leaders take to involve members, ministry team leaders, and church staff will result in buy-in, motivation, and relationships as a church follows God's leadership through the year.

Ongoing Planning

Throughout the year, meetings are needed for evaluation and accountability. With church staff members, evaluation and accountability take place in both structured and unstructured environments. Structured meetings include performance review sessions where staff members go over their *MAPPs* with their supervisors. The *MAPPs* are also used by the personnel committee to consider ways to improve working situations for staff members and evaluate the distribution of resources among staff members.

Weekly staff meetings are the main points of coordination and collaboration. These meetings need to include time for staff members to share stories about how their ministries are implementing their plans and meeting their goals. Many of these stories deserve celebration and recognition of success. The bulk of the time spent in staff meetings needs to be focused on coordination and collaboration that is set in the context of relationships among staff members. When the relationships are strong among staff members, the challenges coming out of coordination and collaboration will be handled in a Christlike manner.

Unstructured opportunities are always useful for building relationships as staff members share what is happening in their ministries and share ideas. These meetings might take place in coffee shops, hallway conversations, and recreational settings such as golf and tennis. Perhaps these unstructured settings provide the best opportunities for strengthening relationships among staff members.

The leadership community members (staff and leaders of the committees and teams) also benefit from ongoing structured and unstructured meetings for coordination and collaboration based on the annual plans. These meetings may take place quarterly in a framework of fellowship, sharing stories, and reviewing the overall plans for the year. As with the staff members, time needs to be set aside for celebrating successes and evaluating what actions are needed to get back on track. These face-to-face meetings strengthen the missional culture of a church by bringing leaders together for intentional coordination and collaboration bathed in fellowship and prayer.

Just as for the staff, unstructured times for members of the leadership community to come together might also take place in coffee shops, recreational settings, social events, and in the hallways. When the leaders of the committees and teams know each other, the list of informal opportunities for coordination and collaboration is endless. These relationships strengthen the church's ability to move toward accomplishing its vision for the future.

The involvement of member ministers could easily be ignored in a conversation about ongoing planning opportunities. However, the spiritual and ministry plans made by individual members are not just words on paper. Member ministers need the opportunity to share their stories, reflecting on what God is doing in their lives, and staying on track with what God had them put on their *MAPPs*. Their structured time for debriefing and collaboration takes place in weekly small group Bible study. The beginning of every Bible study starts with one of the following questions: "What is the best thing that happened to you this week?" "What was the biggest challenge you faced this week?" "What worries you most these days?" or "What about this past week is a cause for celebration?"[179] The unstructured opportunities for members to debrief are endless, including social media. Perhaps these member ministers' conversations are the backbone of a church moving toward accomplishing the vision set before them.

Hence, a dynamic planning system includes a set of actions that take place through ongoing (structured and unstructured/informal) meetings throughout the year for vocational ministers (staff), the leadership team, and individual Christ-followers. The result is a sense of ownership by the church family as a whole.

Conclusion

What if a church family successfully implemented a dynamic planning system? Just imagine what a church family would experience if the majority of members bought into intentional participation in accomplishing the vision and mission of the church. Perhaps the criteria for this level of success can be expressed in two ways. First, everyone senses the leadership of God in the process. Second, everyone has significant opportunities to participate in the planning processes of coordination and collaboration. All generations of adults would find such successes to be compelling reasons to let themselves enjoy their church with a *get-to* attitude rather than a *have-to* attitude.

In summary, this *get-to* attitude is nurtured by an increasingly missional church culture that depends on a relational planning system. This system intentionally involves everyone in accomplishing the church family's vision, focuses on making disciples, thinks strategically, establishes priorities, and sequences activities for accomplishing their goals. The key word here is *their* goals. Not just the pastor and staff goals. This relational planning system gives God the opportunity to empower God's people to participate in meaningful, fulfilling ways that God has gifted them to do individually. The system includes Bible study small groups, leadership communities, and the church staff. The planning actions take place in both structured and unstructured gatherings for framing the vision, annual planning, and ongoing planning through the year.

The purpose of this chapter is to encourage and inspire church leaders to coordinate plans and collaborate with church members through a set of actions to accomplish the mission and vision for a church family. Each church family is challenged to take these ideas as stepping-stones to do what God would have the church do through a relational planning process. What actions would make such a process dynamic for your church? Only God can answer that question. "Many plans are in a man's heart, but the counsel of the LORD will stand" (Proverbs 19:21, NASB).

In Luke 5:4, we find Jesus telling the expert fishermen, "Put out into the deep water and let down your nets for a catch" (NASB). How many of us consider ourselves planning experts based on how we have observed the generations before us do church planning? Perhaps we are finding ourselves in the same place the disciples found themselves that night. We need to let go of what we know and follow God's guidance to let down our nets into the deep water.

Review Questions

1. Why does your church need to plan in the context of relationships?

2. What would relational planning look like in your church?

3. How would planning through coordination and collaboration work in your church?

4. What would happen if your church gradually transitioned to a relational planning strategy that involved everyone in coordination and collaboration processes?

Suggestions for Further Reading

Michael J. Anthony and James Estep, Jr. *Management Essentials for Christian Ministries*. Nashville, TN: B&H Publishing Group, 2005.

George Barna. *The Power of Team Leadership: Finding Strength in Shared Responsibility*. Colorado Springs: Waterbrook Press, 2001.

George Cladis. *Leading the Team-Based Church: How Pastors and Church Staffs Can Grow Together into a Powerful Fellowship of Leaders*. San Francisco: Jossey-Bass, 1999.

Reggie McNeal. *Missional Renaissance: Changing the Scorecard for the Church*. San Francisco: Jossey-Bass, 2009.

Sue Mallory. *The Equipping Church: Serving Together to Transform Lives*. Grand Rapids, MI: Zondervan, 2001.

Will Mancini. *Church Unique: How Missional Leaders Cast Vision, Capture Culture, and Create Movement*. San Francisco: Jossey-Bass, 2008.

Aubrey Malphurs. *Advanced Strategic Planning: A New Model for Church and Ministry Leaders*. Second edition. Grand Rapids, MI: Baker Books, 2005.

———. *Look Before You Lead: How to Discern & Shape Your Church Culture*. Grand Rapids, MI: Baker Books, 2013.

Thom S. Rainer and Eric Geiger. *Simple Church: Returning to God's Process for Making Disciples*. Second edition. Nashville, TN: B&H Publishing Group, 2011.

Robert H. Welch. *Church Administration: Creating Efficiency for Effective Ministry*. Second edition. Nashville, TN: B&H Publishing Group, 2011.

Chapter 10

CONFLICT RESOLUTION IN STAFF AND CONGREGATIONAL RELATIONSHIPS

By Blake Coffee, J.D.

Conflict, for a local church body, is in several respects like waves on the seashore. It is always there at some level. You would never be on your way to the beach and wonder whether there will be any tide today. Of course there will be. Similarly, if there are people in your church, there will be conflict. Whatever conflict you are dealing with today, there is another one behind that, and another one behind that, and so on. If, one day, you go to the beach and there is an eerie absence of any tide at all, watch out—a tsunami is coming! In the same way, a church without any conflict, without any disagreement at all among its people, is—well, a little creepy. In fact, it is one of the symptoms of a spiritually abusive environment.

If the complete absence of conflict is a bad sign, then the presence of conflict is rather a good sign. It means there are people there who are thinking for themselves and who are at least attempting to "work out [their] salvation" together (Philippians 2:12, NASB).

Responses to Conflict

Because conflict is something God obviously permits (that is, God often does not guard us from it), we should be careful about beginning a discussion of conflict by wrongly assigning it some kind of intrinsic negative value. Conflict, in and of itself, is neither a good thing nor a bad thing for a church; it is just *a thing*, a reality, an inevitability. Ultimately, what makes any particular conflict in a congregation a good thing or a bad thing is *how we respond to it.* Any particular conflict with which a church is currently dealing may be the thing that ultimately destroys relationships in that church, or it may be the thing that catapults that church onto a whole new level of ministry. That difference, of course, depends entirely on how the leadership leads the church to respond to the conflict.

Ultimately, what makes any particular conflict in a congregation a good thing or a bad thing is how we respond to it.

Professionals in the work of conflict resolution commonly refer to two negative responses to conflict: *fight* responses and *flight* responses. Both are wrong. Both will cause damage to a church.

Fight responses are those that come from a heart set on causing pain or humiliation. Or, in some cases, they are an ill-conceived response to pain or humiliation. They see *the opposition* as an object rather than as a human being and fellow believer. They tend to

168

exaggerate the differences between us and overlook what we have in common. They do not see the Spirit of Christ in one another; indeed, they cause us to question whether Christ is there in that brother at all. *Fight* responses make us *otherize* and *demonize* each other, as justification for the truly ugly thoughts and feelings we are espousing. They foster a win-lose mentality, wherein winning holds a higher value than the underlying relationship. When we exhibit a *fight* response, we often do so under certain *banners* that seem right to us at the time. We *fight* in the name of lofty ideals such as *truth* or *righteousness* or *mission* or *protecting* the church. These responses may seem right at the time (who can argue with such lofty causes as truth or righteousness or mission?), but the *fight* motive underlying our conduct will only serve to destroy relationships, not to build them.

Interestingly, *flight* responses seem like the opposite of *fight* responses, but they are just a different response that comes from the same heart. They still *otherize* or *demonize* the opposition. They still do not see Christ in that other person. But instead of fighting over the conflict, these responses are all about running from it and are often couched in terms of avoiding conflict. To the extent conflict presents us with a new opportunity to glorify God, a new chance to communicate at a meaningful level with one another, *flight* responses ignore that opportunity. Furthermore, they teach our children to do the same thing. Rather than teaching the value of learning to have difficult conversations, these responses raise up a generation of church leaders who avoid difficult conversations at all costs. Worse yet, *flight* responses ignore the plethora of Scripture that teaches us how to lovingly confront one another and how to gently walk together through difficult conversations.

Every leader must know whether he or she leans naturally toward either of these unhealthy responses to conflict. In the church, a leader's characteristic response to conflict will eventually be reflected across the church body. Where *fight* or *flight* responses are fostered, division and disunity follow.

So, if *fight* or *flight* responses are the wrong responses to conflict in the church, what are the right responses? How can a church leader help his or her church respond to conflict in a way that actually glorifies God? If church wellness is comparable to personal wellness, then we identify two categories of healthy responses to conflict: *proactive* measures for wellness and *reactive* measures. We will discuss these categories one at a time.

I. *Proactive Approaches to Church Conflict*

There are some cultural norms, some relational underpinnings, that are supposed to be a part of the New Testament church but that are not necessarily in line with the cultures of this world. These are some things about which church leadership must be intentional, well *before* any particular conflict comes. Church leaders who learn these values and who then foster them in their churches can bring their congregations a long way toward being prepared to glorify God with how they respond to conflict. Church leaders who do *not* become proficient in these particular norms, who do not hold these values, will only lead in a way that sets the church up for failure when conflict comes.

Focus
The focus of the New Testament church is on Jesus. Everything about it points to Jesus. Its worship points to Jesus. Its conversations point to Jesus. Its programs point to Jesus. Even its governing systems point to Jesus. Everything about the church should be focused on Jesus.

The focus of the New Testament church is on Jesus.

When leadership loses this focus (or permits its people to lose this focus), it finds itself at spiritual odds with its original purpose. It falls out of sync. It is like the confusion your brain feels when your eyes see one environment but your body feels another. We call that *motion sickness*. It is your brain being confused and not able to process the circumstances. Similarly, when the church gets focused on something other than Jesus, confusion sets in. For example, when a church focuses on money and then finds that money will not solve the current conflict, things get chaotic. When a church focuses on its pastor or other leader and then there is a moral failure on his or her part, the church feels lost. When the focus is on musical preferences and a new generation of music lovers comes along, there are seemingly unsolvable problems with worship, and the church feels out of sync.

Church leaders have the responsibility of keeping the people focused. This is never truer than in seasons of conflict. But if this focus is not the cultural norm *before* conflict comes along, it will certainly not be the case in the midst of conflict. In that regard, churches are a bit like tea bags: you do not necessarily know what is inside them until you add some hot water. A church that has been taught to keep its focus on Jesus will look for Jesus, even in the midst of conflict.

How does a leader establish and maintain this focus? He or she does so in every conversation, in every lesson or sermon, in every public and private prayer, in every strategic planning meeting, in every committee meeting, in every hospital visit, in every staff meeting, and in every private moment at home. It is not a strategy; it is a lifestyle. It is a way of being. It is not something a leader teaches with mere words or announcements in the church bulletin. Rather, it is something people learn from watching their leader living his or her life.

Believe this: no matter what kind of leader a church has, no matter his or her style or ultimate effectiveness, the church will focus where he or she focuses. It is a part of the human condition. When church leadership is focused on a legalistic interpretation of

Scripture, that becomes the focus of the church (and often the very environment that same leader must contend with when he or she fails in some way and is in need of grace). When church leadership is focused on politics (national, local, or denominational), that becomes the focus of that church as well, and unmanageable conflict is sure to follow.

In every ministry, every business meeting, every committee, and every endeavor of a church, Jesus must be the focus, and it is incumbent on leadership to constantly be casting vision and strategy that ensures that focus.

Relationships
Although it is true that churches are not buildings or programs but rather are people, that is not the entire truth. Rock concerts and football games are people as well. The Rotary club is people. Political rallies and galas are people. Isn't the church something more than any of those gatherings? Isn't it more than just a collection of people with some common goals? Rather, the church is—should be—radically different from any of those things in two critical aspects: (1) the people in the New Testament church are filled with the Holy Spirit, and (2) the church is completely composed of, and dependent on, the *relationships* between those people.

In the church, the unity of the believers—that is, the relationships among the people—is of the very highest value. In Jesus' prayer for the future church in John 17, it is the only thing he prayed for. At a time when Jesus could have asked his Father in heaven for anything at all that would help the future church, Jesus prayed for unity. He did not pray for doctrinal purity. He did not pray for bold preaching, for beautiful buildings, for inspirational programming, for Spirit-filled worship, not even for the effective spreading of the gospel. He prayed for unity, because he knew all these other things would depend on it.

The church, then, is very much a *fabric* of sorts, held together by thousands of threads intertwined with one another. Every place two threads touch each other is a relationship. Those places, cumulatively, are what will determine the strength of that fabric. Where those relationships are broken or non-existent, the fabric is at risk of ripping further. Attention must be paid to those relationships if the fabric is to be useful for any purposes at all.

Relationships, then, are not just a critical element to church health. They are not just one *vital sign* for the church. They *are* the church. Where relationships are broken, there is no church. Where relationships do not exist, there is no church. Relationships— as we will see in the next section dealing with reactive approaches to conflict in the church—are the vehicle God has

Defeating Gossip

For purposes of church conflict, *gossip* can be defined as *any conversation about someone who is not present and that person is not being edified in that conversation.*

This type of communication kills churches. But the reality is that many churches have institutionalized gossip and have made it a regular part of their systems of communication. For example, personnel committees are often guilty of gossiping as they find themselves talking *about* an employee when they should be talking *to* that employee. Another example is the nominating committee, where members may find themselves bringing negative reports about church members under consideration.

Defeating these patterns of communication requires creating a culture in which they are unacceptable. When you come to me to gossip about someone, I should stop you. I should encourage you to go and talk *to that person*; perhaps I might even offer to go with you.

For many of our churches, this will require a significant culture shift. Culture shifts like this begin with leaders. If the people you lead know that you will never be a part of gossip and that you will not tolerate it around you, that will go a long ways toward shifting the culture of your church in this respect.

given the church to deal with whatever conflicts arise. Where there are no relationships, or where relationships are broken, the church's ability to work through difficult issues becomes horribly hampered at best, and impossible at worst.

Because of this reality, the time to address relationships is before unhealthy conflict arises, because it becomes awfully difficult to get participants focused on relationships in the midst of conflict. Churches that hold relationships in high regard, that continuously teach about relationships, and that constantly equip their people with advanced relationship skills, are much better postured to deal with conflict when it comes.

Communication (*antigossip*)

If relationships are the very fabric of the church, then communication becomes critical, as communication is one of the nurturing elements of relationships. This is not necessarily a reference to churchwide communication, such as newsletters and websites. Much more, rather, this is a reference to the development of God-honoring, biblical communication skills within the context of interpersonal relationships. One of the important proactive measures a church can take to prepare itself for conflict is to develop a culture of biblical communication skills, that is, the ability to confront and to have hard conversations with those with whom one disagrees.

Every church split—every single one—begins at this level. Person *A* says something or does something that injures or causes discontent in Person *B*. According to Scripture, Person *B* has only one recourse—to go to Person *A* and begin to work through that difficulty. But this requires God-honoring, prayerful communication skills. It is difficult, complicated, and often painful. Rather than take this course of action, Person *B* may choose to go to a friend or colleague, Person *C*, and share his or her painful experience or discontent. Note: this will not heal Person *B*; it only multiplies the illness. Now there are *two* people who feel injured or discontent. This type of unhealthy communication continues to spread and eventually begins to happen *on the other side of the issues* out of protection for Person *A*, who feels wrongly treated. The effect of all this unholy communication is the development of camps of opposition. The church is now split, perhaps long before anyone even recognizes it.

Note that this communication pattern eventually crystallizes to a point where there is no communication at all happening *across* the lines of division, and all the communication is happening *up and down* the line of division. This unhealthy communication is seen in the *parking lot meetings* after the committee meetings. It is the secret *prayer meetings* held in homes or local establishments but strictly for people who all agree with one another. It is the e-mail blasts that go out to large distribution lists, but again, mostly to people whom we suspect all agree.

Interestingly, other issues may attach themselves to these lines of division. Months or years later, the original pains and interpersonal issues may be forgotten (or well hidden), and it may well appear that the issues closer to the surface are the problem—doctrinal disputes, leadership styles, and so on. But at the heart of every church split is this culture of unholy communication. Consider this counsel from the Apostle Paul: "Do not let any unwholesome talk come out of your mouths, but only what is helpful for building others up..." (Ephesians 4:29, NIV84). Bringing negative reports *about* someone when we should be talking *to* that person is a direct violation of this counsel from Paul.

The word for this type of negative communication is *gossip*. It is not merely a bad act; it is a culture. It becomes the fuel to every inflamed congregation. It takes issues that should be easily handled within the healthy relationships of a church and magnifies them into impossible situations. Where the culture of a church permits this type of communication, unhealthy conflict is sure to follow. On the other hand, churches who work hard to create an *antigossip* culture by teaching what it looks like and by making it culturally unacceptable are infinitely better equipped to deal with conflict when it comes.

Corporate Prayer

Vibrant, Spirit-filled corporate prayer is becoming more and more marginalized in the modern church culture. That, of course, is a problem to the founder of this revolution we call *church*. Jesus himself said the church was to be a "house of prayer" (Luke 19:46, NIV84). Prayer was never intended to be an ancillary function of the church. It was never intended to be an optional element of the Christian faith that we can opt in or out of at our convenience.

One of the earmarks, one of the identifying features, of churches that do not seem to struggle much with unhealthy conflict is that they have a reputation for praying together. In some respects, this is just a different iteration of the *focus* discussed earlier in this section. But beyond that, there is a logical progression that *the church that prays well together stays well together*. It is very difficult to engage in warfare with a person with whom you kneel week after week and pray.

Certainly, this includes individual prayer. There is much to be said about the value of personal prayer time. But this proactive measure goes beyond individual prayer to also include corporate prayer. The two types of prayer are different. Individual prayer is a gradual process of learning to see the world through God's eyes. However, corporate prayer stretches my understanding of who God is, because I am exposed to my fellow Christian's understanding of God (and he or she to mine). Corporate prayer causes me to lean into relationships with others and to begin to see the church and its issues through their eyes.

Church leaders who help establish a culture of corporate prayer, who hold it up as a high value, worthy of our priorities, are taking a critical step toward creating an environment where the church is ready to respond to conflict in a God-honoring way.

II. Reactive Approaches to Church Conflict

Once it is understood and accepted that conflict in the church is inevitable, how we respond to the conflict becomes the difference maker. Even in churches where the *proactive* culture just described is embraced, conflict will still come. Once it does, and particularly once it grows to an unhealthy level, certain realities and scriptural processes will be needed for us to respond in a way that actually helps the church and honors God. These realities and processes are the *reactive* aspects of responding to conflict in the church.

The Dance

Conflict in the church (or in families or in any other group involving relational dynamics) has three realms or arenas in which our efforts can operate: (1) the surface issues, (2) the emotional issues, and (3) the spiritual issues. All three categories of issues are important to any resolution efforts. The surface issues are where the combatants are most likely focused. Even in cases where the surface issues are clearly not the main problem, the participants will need a process that considers them because those issues may well be the only ones they can see at the moment. The emotional issues are some of the personality-driven issues underlying the surface issues. They take into account hurt feelings and perceptions—and, in some cases, old wounds—that tend to color everything else. Finally, the spiritual issues are usually at the very core of the problems. When dealing with God's people, conflict resolution that does not deal with the spiritual issues will almost always be short-lived and far too fragile to survive the test of time.

It would be wonderfully efficient if the reactive processes could simply move through these three arenas one at a time in a nice, clean, linear fashion. But that is never the case. Any Spirit-led process will necessarily move fairly seamlessly from one realm to the other and then back to the first and then on to the third, and so on. In essence, the process is very much a dance, moving back and forth in step with the Spirit. Nevertheless, for our purposes in this chapter, we will discuss processes in each of these three arenas one at a time.

Surface Issues

It may be obvious to the objective observer in any particular church conflict that the larger, deeper problem is not the surface issue.

Models for Church Mediation

For processes and models, church mediators and congregational interventionists have borrowed considerably from the secular world. For example, the Mennonite Peace Center trains church mediators using models from Family Systems therapy because the congregation shares many dynamics with family systems.

The Baptist General Convention of Texas (through Dr. Nancy Ferrell) has used mediation models from the Department of Justice that deal with neighborhoods and community conflict, for the congregation is very much a community.

The Institute for Christian Conciliation ("Peacemaker Ministries") focuses more on individual reconciliation with a heavy emphasis on scriptural teachings on confession and forgiveness.

Christian Unity Ministries prefers a committee or *elder* approach, forging consensus first in a small, representative group of church leaders who speak from all sides to the issues, and then using that group to form consensus in the larger congregation.

None of these models are wrong, and neither are any of them unscriptural. The right model is the one that fits the church and the issues. An effective process should always consider the cultural and communication norms of the congregation as well as the breadth and complexity of the issues.

Indeed, the surface issue is rarely the real problem. However, in the eyes of the combatants, it is usually the only problem. So, although there is a temptation to sidestep the surface issue to get to the deeper emotional and spiritual issues, the reality may well be that the participants are simply not ready for that. Often, until there is at least some honest and open discussion about the perceived problem (the surface issue), there can be no forward progress at all.

With the Spirit of God indwelling every

believer, God has equipped the church with the vehicle it needs to find its way forward through any surface issues, no matter the complexity or the emotional impact of them. Where relationships are right and scriptural, it is as if the church has the ability to operate with the efficiency of a fine Swiss watch. Those relationships, then, are the very vehicle God has given us to discern solutions to issues.

The problem, of course, is that those relationships are often broken or nonexistent. Add to that dysfunction the complexities of heavy issues such as doctrinal disputes, racial overtones, generational differences, or other such emotionally charged issues, and suddenly "for now we see in a mirror dimly" (1 Corinthians 13:12, NASB) seems like a huge understatement! We can lose our bearings altogether.

Often the first dysfunction that makes this process feel impossible (particularly in the American church) is the false notion that the church is a democracy, existing for the will of the people. We have relied to such a large extent on the democratic process in doing the *business* of the church that we have forgotten that it is not *our* will that ultimately matters but, rather, *God's* will. We have asked *all those in favor* so much that we have begun to believe the majority vote is what governs the church. That, of course, presses the church even further down the already dangerous path of becoming a consumer-driven institution rather than the spiritual revolution it was created to be.

This is not to say that congregational government is in any way a bad system. However, it is important to recognize that, ultimately, even a congregational form of decision making must be aimed at discerning the will of God and not just the will of the people.

In dealing with the surface issues, then, the first objective is to call everyone to the same goal of letting go of what they want in order to pursue what God wants. Obviously, the church that has embraced the *proactive* cultural norms discussed earlier in this chapter has a clear advantage right from the beginning of the *reactive* process. If Jesus is truly the focus of a church, the notion of letting go of what I want is not nearly so difficult. Nevertheless, this must be the first and clearest message of the reactive process: we are pursuing what God wants. Our objective in finding our way forward is to discern the will of God—together.

Scripture gives us several beautiful illustrations of how to find our way through difficult issues and rightly discern the will of God together, but none are clearer and more illustrative than the Jerusalem Council in Acts 15. This, then, will become our backdrop for this topic.

The surface issue dealt with in Acts 15 by the apostles and elders of the church was both complex and emotional. It had critical doctrinal components (the place of circumcision and other Jewish laws and traditions in the gospel and in the lives of the early Christians) as well as racial issues (the coexistence of both Jewish and Gentile believers within the church). It had already been the source of some tension between Peter and Paul as well as among other elders in the Jerusalem church, particularly as those issues pertained to the growing numbers of Gentile converts in the Antioch church. In short, this conflict was huge. There are no conflicts in the church today any bigger or more potentially dangerous than this one was for the early church.

The first lesson we can glean from the Jerusalem Council comes early in that *business meeting*. In Acts 15:7, Luke (the author of Acts) used a phrase we often see in meeting minutes today: "After much discussion" (NIV84). In other words, apparently much said at this meeting did not warrant being placed in the minutes. Things were shared that did not factor into the decision. They may have been emotional outbursts, or they may have been only marginally relevant to the issues. They may well have had more to do with what people wanted than with what God wanted. We do not know. What we do know is that not everything spoken in such circumstances is helpful to the resolution.

As it turned out, the only things that *were* helpful were comments about what God was saying. Specifically, they were all comments about what God was saying through prayer, through circumstances, and through Scripture. First, Peter commented on God speaking through prayer. He reminded the group about what God had said to him while in prayer on the roof of a home in Joppa. Next, Paul and Barnabas commented on what the Spirit was clearly doing among the Gentile believers. Finally, Pastor James commented on what God had said through Scripture. Each of these comments comprised pieces of the larger puzzle. All of them began to form a clear picture of God's will on this very complex issue.

Discerning God's will on the surface issues in a conflict is very much like putting together a jigsaw puzzle. Each prayerfully considered comment and testimony is placed on the table, and all of the pieces are then examined to find how they fit together and what picture they seem to be forming. We still see "in a mirror dimly" when we see only the individual pieces, but the convergence of all the puzzle pieces begins to give us the full picture.

Obviously, this is not a quick process. Neither is it a process to be entered into lightly. It is a prayerful process, requiring much discernment and often some creative thinking. But most of all, it is a process that requires all the participants to let go of the very narrow picture they have in mind so that they can pursue the larger (and most likely very different) picture God has in mind.

In the case of the Jerusalem Council, it was a smaller group of apostles and elders who discerned the way forward. Great attention must be paid to how the recommended resolution was communicated to the rest of the church in that situation. Note that the guiding value in forging that communication was church unity. In other instances, the issue may need a larger group, even the entire congregation. Obviously, the larger the group, the more complicated it becomes to format the process. The governing culture of the church (that is, whether it is a committee-led church, a pastor-led church, or a congregational church, etc.), together with the nature and complexity of the issue(s), will dictate which consensus-building model will work best for that church. But no matter the model, it is always about building consensus and unity.

One of the guiding questions, then, throughout the process of dealing with the surface issues is this: What type of resolution will help hold this church together? It requires creatively pursuing resolutions other than win-lose scenarios. It requires looking for common ground and building on it. It requires listening for the legitimate underlying interests of the parties, rather than the ultimate positions to which those interests give rise, and then crafting possible solutions to meet those legitimate interests.

Finally, the resolution(s) to the surface issues are often the ones that should be reduced to writing. They should include a clear path forward with specific, measurable goals and objectives on behalf of the respective parties (and, in some cases, the entire congregation). A participant's verbal agreement to change a course of action and to meet certain specific guidelines *should* be enough among Christ-followers, but unfortunately, it often is not. There is just something sobering and solemn about reducing the agreement(s) to writing and signing it as a commitment to moving forward. Often, the exercise of choosing the correct language to memorialize an agreement itself reveals some misunderstandings and areas where clarification is needed.

Emotional Issues

These are issues of pain or fear that prevent us from seeing the truth about another person or group of people or set of circumstances—that is, seeing them the way God sees them. It may be unresolved pain from a broken relationship. It may be irrational fear about a group of people with whom I have no relationship at all. It may be old, unresolved pain from traumatic events in my past. Issues from my family of origin often come to bear on my ability to see truth in certain scenarios. In church conflicts, it is very common for a person's ability to cope to be heavily informed by a painful conflict in a previous church.

There are far too many emotional variables and possible issues to try to deal with here. Even things such as temperament and personality types come into play. Suffice it to say, all such emotion-based characteristics and unresolved pain play a significant part in a person's ability to see the truth about another person, group, or set of circumstances. And it is our ability to see the truth that makes working through the surface issues possible. Therefore, although most conflicts must at least begin with an honest discussion of the surface issues in order to allow the parties to move forward, an effective reactive process may also require dealing with some of these emotional issues sooner in the process rather than later—hence, *the dance* referenced earlier.

One emotional issue we will take the time to discuss here is the issue of reconciliation. More specifically, the presence of unresolved pain within a relationship often causes a skewed perspective of the surface issues and requires attention if the parties are to move forward. Unresolved pain is a tool the enemy of the church uses to blind us to the truth, particularly the truth about another person. Unresolved pain can cause even the most spiritually mature person to believe almost any lie about another person. It is necessarily part of the fallout from broken relationships.

Any process designed to bring resolution among God's people must necessarily include a process for healing broken relationships. Specifically, it must be aimed at getting the specific pain identified, articulated, embraced by the other party, and resolved. In short, it means a healthy expression of that pain, an acknowledgment by the *offending party* of the pain caused, an appropriate expression of regret, and an appropriate expression of forgiveness by the injured party. This, of course, is a gross oversimplification of a process that may take many sessions to achieve but that may be critical to a church's conflict resolution, especially if the parties needing reconciliation are key players in the surface issues.

One question worth asking, then, in every church conflict is this: If there is a single relationship within the church that, if miraculously healed, would thereby bring the most resolution to the current conflict, which relationship would it be? If there is a quick and easy answer to that question, then that relationship should probably become a target in the process.

Spiritual Issues

At the very heart of most church conflicts are spiritual issues, which demand spiritual solutions. This requires leadership with a solid working understanding of the whole of Scripture, not just selected verses or passages taken out of context. Scripture (with the assistance of the Holy Spirit) contains all the wisdom a church needs to navigate troubled waters. Any process aimed at addressing the spiritual issues underlying a church's conflict should emanate from Scripture, and any proposed solutions should absolutely line up with Scripture.

This is one of the key differences between secular mediation models and church mediation. The only goal (and the highest value) in secular mediation is the agreement. As long as the parties are in complete agreement, the content of the agreement is not important to the process. In secular mediation, there is rarely any genuine ethical consideration of the proposed solution, as long as all parties are in agreement. But in the church, there is always the question of whether the proposed solution lines up with Scripture. This makes church mediation more *directive* than passive, and it requires that the person(s) facilitating the process have a command of Scripture.

Typical spiritual issues at the heart of church conflict include matters of biblical interpersonal relationships, biblical patterns of communication, biblical models of accountability, and, of course, a commitment (or lack thereof) to prayer. These are all typical spiritual problems, which, if permitted to remain broken and not addressed by a reactive process, will ultimately cause any proposed solution to unravel and conflict to resurface. Thus, churches with a long history of unhealthy conflict are most likely dealing strictly with surface issues and are never addressing the core spiritual problems.

Addressing these spiritual issues is, first and foremost, an educational process. It requires opening Scripture together and allowing the Holy Spirit (through a trusted teacher/communicator/facilitator) to change hearts. It requires gaining a new perspective on old pat-

> ### Sources for Outside Help
>
> - Your denominational entity (local association, national/ state convention, diocese, presbytery, synod, etc.)
> - Christian Unity Ministries (www.christianunityminis-tries.org)
> - Peacemaker Ministries (www. hispeace.org)

terns and being changed by that new perspective. It is the process that Paul described in Romans 12:2: "Do not conform to the pattern of this world, but be transformed by the renewing of your mind" (NIV).

Getting Outside Help

There are several advantages to bringing help in from the outside when dealing with conflict in the church. A fresh, objective set of eyes almost always helps with perspective. Obviously, if you as the pastor or leader in the church are in any way made to be one of the parties to the conflict, an outside perspective becomes critical. Once you are perceived as being one of the parties to the conflict (whether you actually are or not), you will not be effective as a facilitator of a helpful reactive process. In other words, it is essential that all parties perceive the person in charge of the process as being completely neutral. As soon as that neutrality is perceived as being tarnished, the entire process comes into question.

Most professionals working in this field would agree they would prefer to be brought into the conflict earlier rather than later. The earlier they are brought in, the higher the likelihood of a successful resolution. Unfortunately, the longer relationships are broken, the lower the likelihood of the parties being able to see the truth about each other and their circumstances.

The challenge, however, to bringing someone in from the outside, is helping him or her to gain entry into the conflict in the first place. They must be perceived by all the parties as being (1) knowledgeable and competent, and (2) completely neutral. They must have acceptance by key players on all sides to the conflict. They cannot be invited into the conflict by merely one side or the other, and neither can they be perceived by anyone as having clear leanings in any particular direction. In most cases, an outsider gaining entry into the conflict is one of the most delicate steps of the process.

An objective outsider also has a distinct advantage in terms of being the teacher, communicator, and facilitator of spiritual lessons. The unfamiliar style of communication (as opposed to their own pastor's more familiar patterns) may assist the participants in their engagement of the message. Additionally, the objective outsider has an advantage in the process of reducing the ultimate agreement to writing, insofar as there are no credibility issues with the selection of particular words or language to memorialize the agreed-on steps.

Summary

A God-honoring environment for responding to conflict in the church begins long before the conflict arrives. It involves creating a scriptural culture for interpersonal relationships and patterns of behavior and communication. Then, once conflict does surface, a right response involves not only a scriptural approach to the surface issues but also a more holistic approach that addresses the emotional and spiritual issues underlying those surface issues. Finally, much discernment should be exercised in determining whether and when to bring help in from the outside.

Review Questions

1. Which "wrong" response to conflict do you lean toward most naturally, *fight* or *flight*?

2. What is the difference between a proactive versus a reactive approach to conflict? How does one inform the other?

3. What are four cultural norms that help form an effective proactive approach to managing church conflict?

4. What are the three levels of issues to address in an effective reactive process for church conflict? Given your own background and skills, which of these three areas do you believe would be most difficult for you to address? Why?

5. What are the advantages of bringing in an objective outsider to help process church conflict? What are the challenges?

Suggestions for Further Reading

Arbinger Institute. *The Anatomy of Peace*. San Francisco: Berrett-Koehler Publishers, Inc., 2008.

Dietrich Bonhoeffer. *Life Together*. London: SCM Press Ltd., 1954.

Blake Coffee. *Five Principles of Unity*. San Antonio, TX: Christian Unity Ministries, 2010.

Ken Sande. *The Peacemaker*. Grand Rapids, MI: Baker Books, 2004.

Ron Susek. *Firestorm*. Grand Rapids MI: Baker Books, 1999.

Chapter 11

LEADING A CHURCH WHEN MORAL FAILURE OCCURS

By Larry C. Ashlock, Ph.D.

Moral failure is a recurring theme in life. *Les Miserables,* Victor Hugo's masterful work of historical fiction, tells how the benevolent Bishop of Digne took the ex-convict Jean Valjean into his home only to have Valjean steal his silverware. Similar scenes have been relived countless times in actual church experiences, but sadly, the bishop's loving and compassionate response to the sin is not how the story ends in many churches. Churches often place their focus somewhere other than on rescuing the fallen.

Typically, the main emphasis in churches is placed on bearing fruit, not bearing one another's burdens. After all, Christ's followers are exhorted to love one another and hate the evil in the world (John 15:12–13, 17–20; Romans 12:9), and to take up the cross and follow Jesus (Mark 8:34). They are to lead virtuous lives: to be

PASTOR, STAFF, AND CONGREGATIONAL RELATIONSHIPS:

humble (Matthew 5:3; 18:3–4), to be moral influences in the world (Matt. 5:13–15), and to "hunger and thirst for righteousness" (Matt. 5:6, NASB). Greatness for Christ's followers is measured by "ministering servanthood" (see Mark 9:33–36; 10:43–45) and by teaching others to become disciples (Matt. 28:19–20).[180]

Christians are no doubt well-prepared for devotion and duty, but they are too often ill-equipped for disappointment and failure. Therefore, when others fail, the moral influence of a leader cannot be overstated. This truth often passes unnoticed, however, until after a moral collapse occurs in the corporate life of the community of faith.[181] It did not pass the notice of the fictional Bishop of Digne. Rather than censuring the culprit Valjean, he forgave the thief and then exhorted him to use the silver as a means to live an honest life from that point forward. Divine forgiveness and restoration! As Henri Nouwen once said, "The minister is forever making the connection between the human story and the divine story."[182]

The contemporary church moral landscape provides abundant evidence that the body of Christ desperately needs forgiveness and restoration. High-profile sexual, financial, and relational moral failures have scandalized the church, ruined lives, and hindered the influence of the gospel. Too often the church fails to practice biblical discipline *and* renewal *prior to and after* the moral fall of a pastor, prominent leader, or church member. Surely there is a better way to prepare for moral failure and respond to such events in the church body. This chapter will demonstrate that churches respond best to moral failure by applying a holistic biblical model before, during, and following a fall.

The Meaning of Moral Failure

The phrase *moral failure* is not listed, as such, in the *Oxford English Dictionary*, but the meaning of the expression can be clearly determined. The adjective *moral* means "concerned with the principles of right and wrong behavior and the goodness or badness of human character." *Failure* means "an unsuccessful person," "the omission of expected or required action," and "a lack or deficiency of a desired quality."

When the two words are combined, the meaning becomes clear. To fail morally means that a moral principle has been broken by bad behavior. It signals a flaw in character and indicates that not only the individual in question but also others have been adversely affected by the action. Moral failure, then, can be defined as a breakdown of principled behavior through bad motives and wrong action (or inaction). By its very definition, one can see that moral failure is not a private matter.

Moral Failure Affects All People

Fixing Our Eyes on Jesus

The Scriptures record the moral failure of all humanity. Adam and Eve's rebellion in the Garden serves as a reminder of the totality of their (and our) moral fall (Genesis 3; Rom. 3:23). God confronted Adam and Eve in their sin as he did his chosen people throughout Israel's history. In Scripture, from Genesis 3:11 forward, justice (Gen. 3:9–13), mercy (Gen. 3:22–24), and hope (Gen. 3:15) were all features of God's character and action in regard to sin (Exodus 34:6).

The lust of the eyes, the lust of the flesh, and the pride of life describe the totality of human sin (1 John 2:16). If one reads the Scriptures through an ethical lens, one sees evidence of such sins in the lives of prominent Bible characters like Eve (Gen. 3:6), Sarah (Gen. 21), Samson (Judges 13–16), King David (2 Samuel 11:2; 2 Sam. 24), and Ananias and Sapphira (Acts 5). The Scriptures also record the moral victory of Christ, who never fell prey to the lust of the eyes, the lust of the flesh, and the pride of life (Matt. 4:1–11) and did not commit sin (Hebrews 4:15). Christ led by word and deed and sets a proper moral example for leaders to follow.

So Great a Cloud of Witnesses

Christians have known of the importance of good moral behavior from the earliest point in their history, and although space will not permit an exhaustive review of historical emphasis on addressing moral failure in the church, several key sources illustrate its importance. The *Didache*, perhaps the earliest Christian catechism, dating from the late first or early second century, exhorts Christians to behave in a manner that is fitting for a follower of Jesus. Christ and the Scriptures formed the foundation for moral action that was right and good. There are familiar proscriptions against adultery, covetousness, and bearing false witness, as well as warnings to avoid anger, jealousy, being hot-tempered, and lying. It is noteworthy that the *Didache* states, "You shall not hate any man; but some you shall reprove, and concerning some you shall pray, and some you shall love more than your own life."[183] Even while reproving sin, church members were exhorted to love one another, an attitude that mirrors Christ's example.

Even while reproving sin, church members were exhorted to love one another, an attitude that mirrors Christ's example.

Likewise, the early church fathers penned significant documents that provided instructions for pastors on how to lead the church. These writings have served as foundational sources for nearly two millennia. Bishops and pastors were exhorted to model proper behavior and to practice oversight with discipline *and* love.[184]

Martin Luther (1483–1546) longed for Christians to have personal copies of the Scriptures in their own hands and to study them diligently. He worried that people would fall prey to the temptation to read Christian books to the neglect of the study of God's word.[185] Additionally, Luther encouraged a "spiritual priesthood," whereby lay members of a church would study diligently the word of God; instruct others; and "admonish, chastise, and comfort their neighbors" (see 1 Peter 2:9–10). He believed that the failure of lay members to hold one another accountable would lead to disorderly lives.[186]

Philip Jacob Spener (1635–1705) provided post-Reformation believers with solid instructions for exercising proper church discipline. He stressed the importance of not admitting those who made application to join a church until there was reason to believe that they would lead lives worthy of the calling to be a Christian.[187] He also demonstrated a broad approach to strengthening a church, one that would help to guard against moral failures. The word of God formed the basis for all instruction and discipline. Christians were to study the Scriptures privately in their homes, and the church was to provide serious Bible study for its members as well. Spener then urged the formation of "small groups" in the life of a church. Members, led by ministers, would meet together to study the Scriptures, to discuss verse-by-verse their meaning, and to make application to their lives.[188] Spener believed that pastoral involvement was a critical component in the successful growth of Christians. Preachers would establish a bond with their members, learn their strengths and weaknesses, and enable them to grow in doctrine and piety.[189]

Let Us Run the Race with Endurance

Contemporary pastoral leadership and ministry, while acknowledging the importance of various helping acts that provide aid to the church, must remain ultimately accountable to provide *care for souls*. One aspect of soul care is the pastoral function of *reconciliation*. Pastors seek to reestablish broken relationships both between individuals and between people and God. The two modes for this soul repair are forgiveness and discipline.[190] Forgiveness implies that confession has been made, pardon of sin has been received, and a changed life has then followed. The forgiven person is returned to a right relationship with God and with his or her neighbor. Discipline, as a reconciling function, serves to place alienated persons into a situation where "good relationships might be re-established."[191] Simply stated, a pastor must take the lead in modeling, initiating, and sustaining reconciliation in the life of the church.

Simply stated, a pastor must take the lead in modeling, initiating, and sustaining reconciliation in the life of the church.

Pastors also will want to take the lead and set the example for reconciliation with staff members. Churches, for example, unintentionally often set staff members up for moral failure by treating them as persons who have been "hired to do the work of the church."[192] This condition can certainly lead to exhaustion, poor choices, and, perhaps, moral failure.[193] Pastors who shepherd their churches well seek to establish safeguards for staff health. These protections will include time for rest, relaxation, and recreation for staff members and their families.

One would have to be incredibly naïve to believe that moral failure by staff members occurs solely due to overwork. The subject is complex. Studies, however, suggest that a consistent pattern of behavior exists in those who fall due to sexual misconduct, and these behaviors can surface as well with other types of moral failure such as abuse of power.[194] Ministers who fall lack proper supervision, have access and accessibility that lay church members do not have (for example, access to buildings after hours), and the power associated with knowledge (often intimate) of church members.[195] A lack of proper oversight, unobserved personal and professional boundaries, and unhealthy attitudes toward other individuals (for example, narcissism) contribute to ministers' moral failure. Although it

194

would be helpful to establish proper safeguards in staff-layperson relationships (such as to ensure proper counseling protocols), the foundational issue is that the pastor understand and exercise commitment to God for the moral role of "shepherd" for those to whom he has been called to lead and serve (1 Pet. 5:1–4).

Equipping Churches to Prepare for, and Respond to, Moral Failure

Total Church Discipleship

Although it may surprise some, the Bible speaks clearly about the call for *total* church discipleship—inclusive of pastor, staff, and church membership. There is no biblical bifurcation between belief and practice in the church (Matt. 5:6, 13–15, 20). Christ's call involves denying one's self and taking up one's cross (Mark 8:34). The roots of such discipleship are planted in spiritual poverty (Matt. 5:3) and humility (Matt. 18:3–4). Furthermore, discipleship is marked by love for fellow believers (John 15:12–13), faithfulness to Christ's way (1 John 1:5–7), servanthood (Mark 10:43–45), and teaching other disciples (Matt. 28:19–20). When church members and staff together understand their common biblical roles and set up intentional accountability, the church is healthier and less prone to moral failure.

The Importance of Discipline

Whether the sin be dishonesty and pride (Acts 5:1–11; see also Rom. 1:28–32, "deceit"), sexual misconduct (1 Corinthians 5:1–8), or even being a disruption in the life of the church (factionalism, 1 Cor. 1:10–17; Titus 3:10–11), it is abundantly clear that the assembly of God's people is to be disciplined and orderly based on a common respect for God's moral authority ("fear," see Acts 5:5).[196] Discipline includes much more than a response to moral failure; it is also a lifestyle. Disciplined believers answer Christ's call, "Follow me," by living in the Spirit of Christ. In each of the cases of moral failure listed previously, the failure was due to using another person for self-gratification rather than by serving others sacrificially. Biblical discipline in the church grows from members being a disciplined fellowship of believers.

The Primacy of Love and Restoration for the Fallen
The love of Christ is the stream that runs throughout the life of a healthy church. Whether it is a person who has fallen into a sin (Galatians 6:1–5) or one who has acted shamefully (as in the incestuous relationship in 1 Cor. 5:1–8), the goal of the disciplining and reconciling church is to offer the love of Christ, to extend forgiveness to the repentant, and to seek the restoration of the fallen (Matt. 18:21–22; 2 Cor. 2:1–11). When the church deals biblically with moral failure, the result is a vibrant fellowship.

Biblical Guidelines for Dealing with Moral Failure

Individual Moral Failure
Any moral collapse of a pastor is a solemn concern. Paul speaks directly to moral failure on the part of a pastor in 1 Timothy 5:19–20. Here an elder who serves well is worthy of "double honor" (1 Timothy 5:17), and any accusation against the moral character of a pastor is only to be made first privately with the corroborating witness of two to three others; if the pastor refuses to repent, then it is to become a church matter.[197] Moral failure among other believers is also a serious church concern (Matt. 18:15–17). In both instances of pastoral *and* church member moral failure, sin was not to be *swept under the rug* but was to be confronted directly, even if privately at first.[198] The underlying goal in both circumstances is to demonstrate reverence for God and a deep reluctance to sin. The underlying hope is for future repentance and restoration (2 Cor. 2:1–11). It is evident, even from the seriousness of the situation, that *longsuffering* is to be at work, reflecting God's character in such circumstances (Exodus 34:6).

Corporate Moral Failure

Pastors and leaders bear an important burden to remain watchful for moral failure in *the body of Christ*. God disciplined the nation of Israel for its moral collapse before the golden calf (Exod. 32), and the Old Testament prophets spoke against Israel's moral failings both to worshipping God properly and loving its neighbors (for example, Isaiah 1).

Churches are often aware of moral failure on the personal level but are largely blind to the same corporately. God also will discipline his church (Heb. 12:1–13). For example, James warned the church in Jerusalem against the sin of partiality (James 2:1–13), and Paul corrected quarrelsome and boastful behavior at Corinth (1 Cor. 1:10–17) as well as dishonesty and laziness in Crete (Titus 1:12–13). Likewise, contemporary pastors and leaders help the entire church to remain vigilant until Christ returns and to remain alert and on guard by addressing moral concerns affecting the entire body of believers (Ephesians 5:14–16; 6:18).

Ethical Implications of Moral Failure

The Authority of God

The authority of God and Christ has significant meaning in the Scriptures and therefore holds deep implications for ethics. The term *authority* signifies the absolute possibility of action that is fitting for God. When referring to Christ, the word speaks of Christ's divinely given authority (and power) to act and Christ's own rule in "free agreement with the Father." The church requires Christ's "enablement" even to come into existence, and it operates totally under the power and authority of Christ.[199]

The Leader's Spiritual Authority

The relationship of pastor to staff and pastor to church members is of moral importance because the pastor represents a higher, God-given source of authority (1 Pet. 5:1–5). Likewise, all leaders also "embody" a church's "collective identity and continuity, as well as its values and mandate."[200] In this sense, church leaders serve as symbols. Church members often view their leaders as such. A leader may represent "religious truth, the spiritual way of life and perhaps even the reality of God."[201] This representative role endows a minister with great spiritual authority. Furthermore, a leader, by virtue of charisma or personal relationships, can also wield tremendous power in an organization.

Whenever a pastor or church leader abuses his or her authority and power, the consequent moral failure is deeply hurtful, and the harmful effects can often last for years.

Whereas authority gives a person a right to do something, power focuses on the ability to influence others and includes "the possibility of imposing one's own will upon the behavior of other persons."[202] Therefore, in a community of faith, the relationships between leaders and followers must be intentionally exercised in a healthy fashion. Whenever a pastor or church leader abuses his or her authority and power, the consequent moral failure is deeply hurtful, and the harmful effects can often last for years.

Broken Trust
A violation of trust often lies at the root of moral failure. A violation of personal trust occurs whenever a minister is motivated by his or her own needs and uses power to achieve his or her personal ends.[203] On a wider scale, the church is viewed as a *sanctuary*, and leaders are expected to be safe sources of spiritual guidance, love, and forgiveness. However, if a minister exploits personal knowledge of a church member to gain any kind of advantage, then a sacred trust has been compromised. For example, if a pastor

reveals to others the details of a private counseling session in which some sin was confronted or confessed, then a boundary of trust has been breached. If a pastor or leader uses such knowledge to gain an unfair advantage over a church member, then trust has been compromised. Church members trust their pastors to protect their families, but their trust is betrayed when a pastor uses private information in a publicly hurtful way.

Human Dignity in Community

Moral failure impacts human relationships, and it affects human dignity particularly adversely. Humans have been fashioned in God's image to care for God's creation as God cares for us (Gen. 2:15). "We are the image of God...as we mirror God's own nature to the people around us."[204] Because humans have been created in God's image (Gen. 1:26), a violation of personhood occurs whenever misconduct occurs.

The image of God reflected in humans also extends beyond the personal to the social. God created male and female so that they might enjoy *community* with each other. God's divine image is "a shared, corporate reality, which is present only in community."[205] The perfect example of community is the triune God. The Godhead, comprised of Father, Son, and Holy Spirit, is a loving fellowship, and we ourselves can show the *relational reality* of God in our loving relationships. God's love is self-giving, in that it seeks the benefit of others. Christ's disciples are therefore to resemble the fellowship that characterizes *Trinitarian Persons*. Subsequently, any broken relationship mars in some degree, the divine image.

Noting the special trust that has been placed in the pastoral office, an act of moral failure by a pastor or other minister takes on an added dimension. Pastors guide a church in "being a people who live as the image of God, and they trust that their spiritual leader will model God's self-giving love in his (or her) relationships with them."[206] Any violation of the sacred trust between a pastor and the people impacts the human dignity of every individual as it disrupts the community created in God's image.

Justice

The term *justice* is a key word in Christian ethics, and the notion of right conduct, as judged by divine standards, is inherent in its meaning. The virtue of treating others fairly is an important aspect of the term. The root for such attitudes and actions is the character and nature of a Holy God, whose will is for humankind to practice justice. An abuse of ministerial or leadership authority also then impacts justice.[207] As the devastating effects of injustice deeply wound people, healthy churches will choose to pursue fairness, in love, whenever moral failure occurs.

The Importance of Preparedness

The significance of moral failure challenges leaders to make adequate preparation for church wellness *before* such an incident occurs in the life of its body. Leaders also should *prepare policies that outline responses to the various issues involved in moral failure* (for example, sexual misconduct).[208] Certainly, the biblical passages cited earlier in this chapter will serve as a guide for handling moral failure. Furthermore, churches should act without delay when a credible complaint of moral failure surfaces.[209] Once again, the Scriptures provide a basis for approaching a church member who has been accused of some sin. Also, a mature congregation will take seriously any true instance of clergy moral failure such as sexual misconduct or abuse of power (see 1 Tim. 3:1–13; James 3:1; 1 Pet. 5:1–4). Finally, in each of these circumstances a church does well to reflect continually on its own "internal working as a church family."[210]

The high incidence today of clergy and church member misconduct suggests the importance of *preparing future ordained and lay church leaders in handling moral failure.* Theological education will certainly include training in the warning signs of susceptibility and pathways to avoid moral failure. Denominations also will provide training to better equip churches to address moral failures before and after they occur. Many denominations, having learned from the moral scandals that have rocked their congregations, such as the Roman Catholic Church, are taking the lead in assembling lists of the individuals who have been identified as sexual predators in previous places of ministry. These denominational groups, as well as other churches and denominations, could also include a watch list of those individuals who have caused harm through other forms of moral failure as well. It is not sufficient only to point out those who have fallen. Denominations will want to provide clear support for the victims. At the same time, religious bodies will also want to provide ministries for offenders with the aim of forgiveness and restoration. The goal would be to reclaim the person for the cause of Christ, not necessarily to restore the person to leadership. [211]

Conclusion

Victor Hugo's *Les Miserables* displays a key theme—resurrection. The fictional character Jean Valjean took the new life offered to him by the saintly bishop and spent the balance of his own life sowing seeds of love and compassion into countless other lives. The true model for addressing moral failure in the life of the church, however, is the example of Jesus Christ (John 8:1–11; Acts 9:13–15; 1 Tim. 1:15), on which the fictional character to an extent was based. Likewise, the biblical methods to address moral failure demonstrated in this chapter are evident from history as well. When utilized by churches, as has been proven through the ages, God's authority is confirmed, trust in God's leaders is restored, human dignity and personhood is protected, and in all cases justice and righteousness is preserved.

Stable churches reflect the marks of such discipleship and discipline. They emphasize the Lordship of Christ (the proper source of authority), the serious study of the word of God, accountability to one another, and a fair and loving response to moral failure that is characterized by the desire to see the sin confessed and the sinner forgiven and restored to the community of faith. When moral failure is addressed, the broken and fallen can be reconciled to useful service in God's kingdom.

Review Questions

1. The marks of a disciplined church have been outlined in this chapter. How many of these marks are evident in your personal walk and in the life of your church? What steps might you undertake to improve discipline in your life and church?

2. List several present personal attitudes or actions that warn you of an impending moral failure. What steps might you put into place personally and corporately to guard against moral failure? How can staff members be helped to guard against moral failure?

3. Review your present church policies regarding moral failure. Outline several steps to strengthen them.

4. Review the denominational resources available to your church for addressing moral failure and to warn against known sexual predators.

Suggestions for Further Reading

Ray Carroll. *Fallen Pastor: Finding Restoration in a Broken World*. Folsom, CA: Civitas Press, 2011.

Richard M. Gula. *Ethics in Pastoral Ministry*. New York: Paulist Press, 1996.

Joe E. Trull and James E. Carter, *Ministerial Ethics: Moral Formation for Church Leaders*. Second edition. Grand Rapids, MI: Baker Academic, 2004.

Earl Wilson. *Steering Clear: Avoiding the Slippery Slope to Moral Failure.* Downers Grove, IL: InterVarsity Press, 2002.

Earl and Sandy Wilson, Paul and Virginia Friesen, and Larry and Nancy Paulson. *Restoring the Fallen: A Team Approach to Caring, Confronting and Reconciling.* Downers Grove, IL: InterVarsity Press, 1997.

Appendix I.

JOB DESCRIPTIONS

By Robby Barrett, D.Min.

Job Description for Pastor

First Baptist Church, Amarillo, Texas

General Description: The pastor provides spiritual, pastoral, and administrative leadership to equip the staff and congregation of First Baptist Church to carry out the Great Commission. The pastor is responsible to proclaim, teach, and share the gospel of Christ, both in word and deed, and provides overall leadership for church ministries and pastoral care.

Primary Responsibilities:

- Plan and conduct worship services, prepare and deliver sermons, lead in observance of ordinances.
- Lead the church to faithfully share the good news of Christ through evangelism and outreach ministries.
- Provide pastoral care for members and prospects.
- Train and assist staff, deacons, and church members to carry out the mission and vision of First Baptist Church.
- Provide pastoral counseling for church members.
- Officiate at special services such as wedding ceremonies and funerals.
- Serve as moderator for church business sessions.
- Cooperate with denominational and sister church leaders in matters of mutual interest and concern.
- Represent First Baptist Church in community and civic matters.
- Promote biblical stewardship of God's resources.
- Oversee and work in conjunction with staff members for administration of all ministries and financial/business affairs.
- Other tasks as needed to strengthen and grow the body of Christ.

Job Description for
Executive Pastor

Oakwood Baptist Church, New Braunfels, Texas

Objective: To provide day-to-day management and oversee the spiritual, emotional, and relational health of the pastoral ministers and other staff as needed. This position will work with the senior pastor to focus attention on the vision and direction of the church.

Reports To: See organizational chart.

Education: High school diploma or equivalent. Bachelor's degree, seminary, and experience desired.

Skill: Strong leadership skills and a strategic thinker who will assist pastoral staff in casting vision and accomplish ministry goals. Experience in supervising and mentoring staff. Ability to teach/ preach as needed.

Job Summary:

- Work with the senior pastor and other leadership to carry out vision and direction for church.
- Provide supervision for staff. Work with executive administrator to ensure that all staff are aware of their responsibilities. Help set vision, direction, and execution of goals for each ministry.
- Assist in the hiring and dismissal of staff as needed. This will include making salary reviews and recommendations as needed.
- Create and maintain all aspects of small group Bible studies. This will include recruiting teachers and determining curriculum needs. Oversight of all elected or specialty groups. This will also include providing leadership to ministry teams as needed.
- Maintain financial oversight in all ministry areas. Submit and approve budget request from ministries that report to the executive pastor.
- Ability to perform weddings, funerals, baptisms, and communion when called upon and other religious ceremonies as needed and appropriate.
- Any and all other matters necessary to further the mission and purpose of the church.

Job Description for
Executive Administrator

Oakwood Baptist Church, New Braunfels, Texas

Objective: To ensure that all business affairs of the church are conducted in a Christlike and professional manner. This position will focus on daily operations as well as resource management.

Reports To: See organizational chart.

Education: High school diploma or equivalent. Bachelor's degree or experience in a business-related field desired.

Skill: Must have an understanding of church stewardship and finance. Knowledge regarding facilities management and maintenance. Must set a professional and caring tone for the church office. Strong management and leadership skills.

Job Summary:

- Work with senior pastor and other leadership to carry out the vision and direction for church.
- Provide supervision for staff. Work with executive pastor to ensure that all staff members are aware of their responsibilities. Help set vision, direction, and execution of goals for each ministry.
- Oversight of all financial aspects of the church. This will include all contributions, payroll, and general accounting functions necessary to operate in a professional manner. This will also include an understanding of all federal and state laws that must be complied with. Provide monthly financial reports to membership and budget/finance team.
- Management of all church facilities. Supervising the maintenance and security of buildings, grounds and equipment.

This will include scheduling the use of facilities, maintaining the church calendar, and setting fees for community events.

- Must seek to maximize all church resources enabling personnel and volunteers to achieve the church's stated goals.
- Must ensure that all business affairs of the church enhance and enable effective ministry.
- Any and all other matters necessary to further the mission and purpose of the church.

Job Description for Associate Pastor

First Baptist Church, Amarillo, Texas

Reports To: Pastor.

General Description: Provide assistance to pastor and staff in meeting pastoral care, preaching and teaching, and mission needs of First Baptist Church.

Primary Responsibilities:
- Preach when pastor is away or when requested.
- Oversee hospital visitation ministry.
- Respond to pastoral emergencies.
- Make regular visits to homebound members.
- Officiate at weddings and funerals as requested.
- Provide pastoral counseling as needed.
- Follow up with people who have suffered the recent loss of a family member.
- Serve as staff liaison with missions committees and to mission churches.
    o Organize and lead mission events, activities, and trips (both local and international).

      o   Encourage congregational participation in mission ministries.
- Teach weekly Bible studies as needed.
- Seek outreach and evangelism opportunities.
- Assist other staff members in development of discipleship ministries.
- Assist with media presentations as needed during worship services.
- Perform other tasks as assigned by pastor.

Job Description for
Minister of Music

First Baptist Church, Amarillo, Texas

Reports To: Pastor.
General Description: Provide overall leadership for worship and a comprehensive music ministry of First Baptist Church.

Primary Responsibilities:
- Lead the planning, organizing, conducting, and evaluating of a comprehensive music ministry including choirs (all ages), vocal and instrument ensembles, and worship leaders/guests.
- Assist the pastor in planning and leading weekly worship services.
- Assist with general ministerial tasks such as hospital visitation, outreach, and care.
- Enlist and train music ministry leaders for choirs, ensembles, and other areas of responsibility as needed.
- Arrange and provide music for funerals, weddings, and other church-related worship experiences.
- Maintain music equipment, supplies, music library, and additional resources.

- Support mission activities and involvement through the church's music ministry.
- Submit and administer the music ministry annual budget.
- Oversee, guide, and evaluate the ministry of the associate minister of music and other music ministry personnel.
- Perform other tasks as assigned by pastor.

Job Description for Minister of Education

First Baptist Church, Garland, Texas

Summary: To provide leadership for the development, coordination, and effectiveness of the overall Christian education ministries of the church.

Reports To: Senior Pastor.

Minimum Qualifications: Christian education (CE) related seminary master's degree preferred and at least seven years of effective local church experience in a similar ministry role in church(es) with similar ministry philosophy, structure, and direction as First Baptist Garland.

Duties/Responsibilities

- Coordinate the work of the education staff team (ministers, directors, and support staff).
    - Help set the vision, purpose, and direction of the overall Christian education ministry.
    - Work with education staff to interpret this vision/ purpose/direction for each age division.
    - Coach the education staff in providing effective leadership to their teams of paid and volunteer leaders.

- o Provide consistent communication regarding progress and issues related to each age division.
- o Ensure needs for space, equipment, and resources are sufficiently anticipated, planned for, and met for all age divisions. (This includes coordination with other staff members outside the education staff team.)
- Give specific direction to the adult education ministries of the church.
  - o Recruit, train, and encourage leaders in the Sunday School/Open Group ministries, discipleship ministries, and any other Christian education ministries for adults.
  - o Ensure curriculum, supplies, and resources are provided.
  - o Communicate vision/purpose/direction (noted above) with applicable adult Christian education leaders.
- Serve as staff liaison for men's ministry leadership.
  - o Be available to provide support and consultation to volunteer leaders in this area regarding planning and coordination of their ministry efforts.
  - o Provide input on the Christian education-related functions of this ministry.
- Give direction for the church's overall outreach/evangelism ministry efforts.
  - o Evaluate and implement improvements as necessary.
  - o Ensure the Great Commission mandate is being maintained as a key ingredient of all ministries in some form.
  - o Model, encourage, and equip others to be a witness in their personal circles of contact and influence.
- Implement and oversee the church's assimilation process for new church members.

- Maintain professional awareness and expertise in the field of Christian education.
- Other duties assigned by supervisor.

Job Description for Pastoral Care and Senior Adult Minister

First Baptist Church, Garland, Texas

Reports To: Senior Pastor.

Summary: Provides leadership and support to pastoral ministries assisting the pastor and effectively leading senior adult ministries.

Minimum Qualifications: Job-related experience, college or seminary, five years' experience in ministry area.

Duties/Responsibilities:

- Pastoral ministries—assistant to the senior pastor
  - o Pulpit ministry as assigned by the pastor
  - o Hospital ministry visitation coordination
    - Coordinate staff ministers' visitation schedule
    - Daily hospital visitation
    - Emergency and presurgery visitation
    - Daily hospital report
  - o Weddings and funerals (average forty to fifty per year)
  - o Counseling (wedding/family/crisis)
  - o Supervise intercessory prayer ministry (IPM) and annual IPM Banquet
  - o Coordinate Wednesday evening service prayer guide
- Senior adult weekday ministry

- o   Coordinate/teach adult Vacation Bible School
- o   Coordinate and supervise senior adult trips
- o   Coordinate annual fiftieth wedding anniversary recognition
- o   Supervise Keenagers
- o   Senior adult game time
- o   Direct grief ministry
- o   Coordinate homebound/nursing home ministry
- o   Oversee homebound bus ministry
- o   Senior adult activities
- Adult discipleship and support groups
  - o   Teach adult discipleship classes
  - o   Direct grief support ministry
  - o   Ushers (training/coordination)
  - o   Decision counselors at worship services
  - o   Liaison to senior adult Sunday School departments
  - o   Provide coordination and support for Sunday School department directors
  - o   Coordinate other special events and meetings
- Other duties as assigned by supervisor

Job Description for
Minister of Young Adults

First Baptist Church, Amarillo, Texas

Reports To: Minister of Education.

Supervises: Minister of Young Adults Assistant.

General Description: Administers the young adult ministry of First Baptist Church.

Primary Responsibilities:

- Oversee the young adult Bible study ministry of First Baptist Church. This includes:
    - o Enlisting, training, and evaluating volunteer workers.
    - o Organizing classes and departments for ministry and growth.
    - o Providing resources such as curriculum, space, and equipment.
- Provide discipleship and growth opportunities for young adults, including:
    - o Sunday and weekday discipleship and Bible study opportunities
    - o Special activities such as evening and weekend seminars
    - o Small groups
    - o One-on-one mentoring
- Maintain an extensive young adult outreach ministry.
- Administer the young adult ministry budget.
- Develop and oversee mission opportunities and projects for young adults.
- Provide continual support and resources for young adult needs, including:
    - o Marriage preparation and enrichment
    - o Financial stewardship
    - o Dating
    - o Time management
    - o Parenting
- Assist minister of education in overseeing men's and women's ministries.
- Provide retreats, fellowships, and other opportunities for young adults to grow in relationship to Christ and one another.
- Regularly communicate young adult activities, events, and ministries to the church family.

PASTOR, STAFF, AND CONGREGATIONAL RELATIONSHIPS:

- Coordinate special projects and activities as assigned by the minister of education.
- Assist the pastor and staff in carrying out the mission of First Baptist Church of Amarillo.
- Other tasks as assigned by minister of education or pastor.

Job Description for Small Group Pastor

Oakwood Baptist Church, New Braunfels, Texas

Objective: To create and maintain host home study groups that support the five purposes of the church (worship, fellowship, discipleship, ministry, and missions).

Reports To: See organizational chart.

Education: High school diploma or equivalent. Bachelor's degree, seminary, and experience desired.

Skill: Strong leadership skills and ability to work well with people. Must have excellent understanding of biblical principles and teachings. Ability to develop strong relationships with Bible study and host home leaders as well as the congregation.

Job Summary:

- Provide support and training to host home leaders.
- Work in conjunction with Discovering Oakwood to help new members be placed in host homes.
- To implement a strategy for the development of new leaders to start new host homes.

- To provide resources and approved teaching material for host homes.
- Attend meetings and events as deemed necessary by supervisor.
- Maintain financial oversight in areas of responsibility.
- Any and all other matters necessary to further the mission and purpose of the church.

Job Description for Minister to Students

First Baptist Church, Garland, Texas

Summary: To develop, organize, and provide leadership for ministry to students (middle school, high school) and their families.

Reports To: Minister of Education.

Minimum Qualifications: Bachelor's degree required; completion or current enrollment toward a seminary master's degree preferred in a field related to youth or student ministry and at least five years of effective local church experience in a similar ministry role in church(es) with similar ministry philosophy, structure, and direction as First Baptist Garland.

Duties/Responsibilities:

- Set the vision, purpose, and direction of the student ministry.
- Develop and manage the student ministry budget.
- Oversee the weekly programming of the student ministry including Sunday School, discipleship, and outreach.
  - o Recruit, train, support, and supervise teachers, helpers, interns, and ministry assistant.

- o Manage annual student/youth Sunday School promotions.
- o Coordinate outreach in conjunction with overall church efforts.
- Plan, promote, and conduct special events related to students/youth and their families.
  - o Summer camps, mission trips, seasonal outreach and fellowship activities and events.
  - o Coordinate follow-up to these events.
- Develop trust and credibility with students and their parents by spending time outside of organized events building relationships for ministry, including:
  - o Minister to families of students/youth during special life events (illnesses/hospitalizations, deaths, etc.).
  - o In partnership with other education staff members, offer customized parenting support for parents of teens.
  - o Coordinate and communicate with related church staff regarding overlapping ministry contacts with teens and their families (for example, youth choir ministry, recreation ministry).
- Ensure all aspects of the church's risk management plan are observed for youth/student ministry activities.
- Maintain professional awareness and expertise in the field of youth and student ministry.
- Other duties as assigned by pastor.

Job Description for Children's Minister

First Baptist Church, Garland, Texas

Summary: To develop, organize, and provide leadership for ministry to children (grades 1–5) and their families.

Reports To: Minister of Education.

Minimum Qualifications: Job-related bachelor's degree required; master's degree preferred. At least five years' experience leading a children's ministry in a church.

Duties/Responsibilities:
- Set the vision, direction, and purpose of the children's ministry.
- Oversee weekly programming for children, including Sunday School, discipleship, missions education, and divorce care for kids.
  - o Recruit, train, and supervise lay leadership, interns, and ministry assistant.
  - o Provide curriculum, supplies, and resources.
  - o Coordinate outreach in conjunction with overall church efforts.
- Serve as codirector for the annual Vacation Bible School in coordination with the preschool minister.
- Plan and supervise the annual preteen camp.
- Plan, promote, and conduct special events for children and their families resulting in fellowship opportunities, discipleship, and growth of the children's division, including:
  - o Develop and oversee children's ministry budget.
  - o Provide individual ministry to children and parents for the following: salvation, parenting, hospitalization, and referrals.
  - o Maintain resource rooms in coordination with the preschool minister.
  - o Maintain professional awareness and expertise in the field of childhood education.
  - o Promote the children's ministry via all available avenues, including internal and external publications and website.

- Ensure all aspects of church's risk management plan are observed for children's ministry activities.
- Participate with the church's education staff in weekly meetings and provide assistance with special events that include children and their families.
- Other duties as assigned by supervisor.

Job Description for Preschool Minister

First Baptist Church, Garland, Texas

Summary: To develop, organize, and provide leadership for ministry to preschoolers, kindergarteners, and their families.

Reports To: Minister of Education.

Minimum Qualifications: Job-related bachelor's degree required, master's degree preferred. At least five years' experience leading a preschool ministry in a church.

Duties/Responsibilities:

- Set the vision, purpose, and direction of the preschool ministry.
- Develop and manage the preschool ministry budget.
- Lead the weekly programming of the preschool ministry, including Sunday School, worship care, discipleship, and mission education.
    - o Recruit, train, support, and supervise teachers, greeters, coordinators, interns, and ministry assistants.
    - o Provide curriculum, supplies, and resources.
    - o Coordinate outreach in conjunction with overall church efforts.

- Oversee the church childcare and weekday education ministries.
- Plan, promote, and conduct special classes and other events related to preschoolers and their families.
- Serve alongside the children's minister as codirector of Vacation Bible School.
- Work together with the entire ministerial team to plan, prepare for, and conduct the fall festival.
- Minister to families during special life events (births, illnesses/hospitalizations, deaths, etc.).
- Offer individual parenting support.
- Promote and maintain a high level of safety, security, and visual appeal in the preschool area.
- Supervise maintenance of resource rooms.
- Maintain professional awareness and expertise in the field of preschool and kindergarten education.
- Other duties as assigned by supervisor.

Job Description for Mother's Day Out Director

First Baptist Church, Garland, Texas

Summary: To provide leadership to the Mother's Day Out ministry

Reports To: Preschool Minister.

Minimum Qualifications: Evidence of strong Christian character; high school diploma; at least three years' experience in childcare

Duties/Responsibilities:
- Set the vision, purpose, and direction of the Mother's Day Out ministry.
- Develop and manage the Mother's Day Out budget.

- Promote and maintain a level of safety, security, and visual appeal in the Mother's Day Out classrooms.
- Hire, support, and provide training for teachers.
- Oversee the publicizing of Mother's Day Out, with a vision for growth.
- Plan, promote, and conduct special events for the Mother's Day Out families.
- Minister to families during special life events such as births, illnesses/hospitalizations, deaths.
- Maintain professional awareness and expertise in the field of preschool childcare and education.
- Other duties as assigned by supervisor.

Job Description for Director of Counseling

Oakwood Baptist Church, New Braunfels, Texas

Objective: To implement and direct a counseling center that ministers biblical, professional, and affordable counseling to members of Oakwood, the Bluebonnet Association, and the community at large.

Reports To: See organizational chart.

Education: This position requires a master's degree or higher in counseling, psychology, social work, or a mental health–related filed. Must be licensed by the State of Texas.

Skill: This position will supervise all counselors and set vision and direction for the counseling ministry. Must communicate effectively with clients, church membership, and contract therapist. Supervision, communication, and counseling emphasis.

Job Summary:

- Provide individual, marital, family, and group therapy as needed.
- Hire and supervise contract counselors, interns, administrative support, and support group leaders. This will include peer review meetings as needed.
- Assign caseload to contract counselors or interns as deemed appropriate.
- Manage all record keeping. This includes billing and receiving as well as confidential client charts.
- Supervise and establish new support groups as needed.
- Provide vision and develop structure for the counseling ministry to grow and meet present and future demands.
- Any and all other matters necessary to further the mission and purpose of the church.

Job Description for Information Technology Manager

Oakwood Baptist Church, New Braunfels, Texas

Objective: To plan, direct, manage, and oversee the activities and operation of information technology at Oakwood Baptist Church and develop an overall strategy using information technology to support Oakwood's mission and core objectives.

Reports To: See organizational chart.

Education: High school diploma or equivalent.

Skills: Must have strong knowledge of all aspects of computers and be well-rounded in software application. Must be detail-oriented and decisive, with the ability to organize and coordinate work, set priorities, and assist others. Must demonstrate strong leadership with the overall church picture in mind.

Job Summary:

- Develop and implement an information technology strategy that helps the church achieve its goals and objectives. This includes maintaining all church computers and network.
- Research and approve expenditures for equipment. This will include computers, sound equipment, lighting, and so on.
- Responsible for researching and evaluating new technologies.
- Work with multiple staff and volunteers. Recruit and train assistants when necessary.
- Leadership and direction of website design and direction. Ultimate responsibility of website.
- Maintain financial oversight in information technology ministry. This will include budget preparation, check requests, and approval of all expenditures.
- Any and all other matters necessary to further the mission and purpose of the church.

Appendix II.

NOTES ON PERSONNEL POLICIES

By Robby Barrett, D.Min.

Personnel policies communicate the way a church calls staff members, administers staff policies, utilizes personnel resources, sets expectations for conduct, and shares a variety of additional information related to employment. Personnel policies are valuable to both the church and the employee in setting clear guidelines and expectations at the beginning of employment and avoiding potential difficulties that may arise later due to unclear communication.

Personnel Committee Purpose, Duties, and Membership (Sample)

Purpose: To assist in the staffing of ministerial, program, and support positions; adopting and implementing personnel policies; overseeing the management of staff; and serving as liaison between the staff and church membership.

Length of Term: Three years.

Rotating: Yes.

Standing or Special: Standing.

Staff Liaison: Pastor.

Duties:

1. Establish, maintain, and publicize policies and procedures for the assigned area of responsibility.

2. Study the need for additional personnel.

3. Develop and keep current all position descriptions.

4. Oversee and recommend to the church the staffing of all ministerial/program positions with the exception of the position of pastor.

5. Recommend search committees, if needed, for staff search (with the exception of pastor search committee).

6. Develop and utilize personnel policies to oversee the management and termination of all employees.

7. Maintain a salary and benefits plan.

8. Develop and recommend an annual budget request to the finance committee as needed. Work with the staff liaison in administering the approved budget.

9. Serve as liaison between the staff and church membership.

Below is a general outline for personnel policies. These are based on the personnel policies of the First Baptist Church, Amarillo, Texas, and the Heights Baptist Church, Richardson, Texas.

General Employment Information

- Classifications of employment
- Orientation for new employees
- Job performance
- Conduct expectations
- Wage and hour definitions
- Compensation
- Employment at will
- Employee counseling

Employment Practices

- Background check
- Work schedules and breaks
- Performance evaluation
- Termination
- Grievance procedures
- Disciplinary action
- Confidentiality
- Outside employment

Benefits

- Vacation
- Holidays
- Illness
- Other absence from work
- Insurance
- Employee recognition
- Housing and automobile allowance

- Relocation expense
- Retirement plan
- Expense reimbursement
- Overtime policy
- Garnishments
- Extended leave of absence
- Jury duty
- Severance pay
- Disability
- Social security

Work Environment

- Electronic and social media policy
- Intellectual property rights
- Fiscal procedures
- Cell phone policy
- Building security and employee safety
- Policy against harassment, discrimination, and retaliation
- Minor safety and employment
- Smoking, alcohol, and illegal drug policy
- Accidents/injuries
- Damage to church property
- Use of church property
- Office closing for weather/emergencies
- Conduct and appearance

Notes

Chapter 1

[1] John Grabner, "Ordained and Lay: Them-Us or We?" *Worship* 54 (1980): 326.

[2] "The history of the church contains a long, sad story of how the gifts and graces and duties which were once part of every Christian's baptismal inheritance were gradually given to the ordained Christians alone. I fear that the current call for a special clerical spirituality could be the latest episode in the ever present tendency to clericalize the church." William H. Willimon, "The Spiritual Formation of the Pastor: Call and Community," *Quarterly Review* 3 (1983): 33.

[3] Os Guinness labels the Catholic two-class system as "the Catholic distortion." Quoted in Chris R. Armstrong, "Refocused Vocation: Over the Centuries It's Been Distorted, but History Also Sharpens Our View of Every Christian's Calling," *Leadership Journal* 1 (2013): 46.

[4] Chris R. Armstrong, "Refocused Vocation," 48. See also Alice R. Cullinan, *Sorting It Out: Discerning God's Call to Ministry* (Valley Forge, PA: Judson Press, 1999), 7.

5 Dan Kimbell, "Calling All Christians," *Leadership Journal* 1 (2013): 94.

6 Cullinan, *Sorting It Out*, 2.

7 Cullinan, *Sorting It Out*, 10–11.

8 Herschel Hobbs, *The Baptist Faith and Message* (Nashville: Convention Press, 1971), 75.

9 William H. Willimon, *Pastor: The Theology and Practice of Ordained Ministry* (Nashville: Abingdon Press, 2002), 17.

10 It is rare to find a church budget that does not devote more than half of the church's resources toward personnel costs. I conducted a recent survey of fifteen large churches in Texas and found the portion of the budget dedicated to personnel expenses ranges from 43.6 percent to 59.5 percent, with an average of 50.6 percent.

11 Michael Kelly, "Having Job Titles That No One Understands" (March 26, 2010), accessed August 20, 2013, www.jonacuff.com/stuffchristianslike/2010/03/having-job-titles-that-no-one-understands.

12 Derek Tidball, *Ministry by the Book: New Testament Patterns for Pastoral Leadership* (Downers Grove, IL: InterVarsity Press, 2008), 190.

13 Leon Morris, *The Epistle to the Romans* (Grand Rapids, MI: Eerdmans, 1988), 51–52.

14 Robert Dale, *Pastoral Leadership* (Nashville: Abingdon Press, 1990), 25.

15 For evidence of and discussion concerning the laying on of hands as associated with the rite of baptism in Baptist churches, see Ernest A. Payne, "Baptists and the Laying on of Hands," *Baptist Quarterly* 15 (1954): 203–15. Alan Kreider, an Anabaptist, has predicted the church will increasingly view baptism as functional ordination. Alan Kreider, "Abolishing the Laity: An Anabaptist Perspective," accessed August 20, 2013, http://www.anabaptistnetwork.com/files/Abolishing%20the%20Laity.pdf.

16 John E. Skoglund, "Rethinking Ordination," *Foundations* 12 (1969): 100.

17 Ordination is a separate but related issue. For a full study on Baptists and ordination, see Howard K. Batson, "Pastoral/Lay Ministry Concerns in Ordination," in William H. Brackney, *Baptists and Ordination: Studies Conducted by Baylor University and the Baptist General Convention of Texas* (Macon, GA: National Association of Baptist Professors of Religion, 2003), 157–175.

18 Alton H. McEachern, *Set Apart for Service* (Nashville: Broadman Press, 1980), 52.

19 McEachern, *Set Apart for Service*, 52.

20 William L. Lumpkin, "The Baptist Doctrine of the Ministry," *Review and Expositor* 55 (1958): 253.

21 Martin Luther, "Concerning the Ministry," in *Luther's Works* (Philadelphia: Muhlenberg Press, 1958), II, 11. For an extended discussion of the varying positions on ordination, especially in the Lutheran tradition, see Roy A. Harrisville, *Ministry in Crisis: Changing Perspectives on Ordination and the Priesthood of All Believers* (Minneapolis: Augsburg Publishing House, 1987), 11–20. Harrisville found contemporary Lutherans at both the sacramental and the functional poles of the ordination debate. John Calvin, in a similar fashion, rejected all sacramental understandings of the ordination process. Calvin depicted ordination as "a sign of offering to God him whom they were receiving into the ministry." John Calvin, "Institutes of the Christian Religion," 4.13.16, *Library of Christian Classics* (Philadelphia: Westminster Press, 1960), XXXI, 67.

22 E. Glenn Hinson, "Ordination in Christian History," *Review and Expositor* 78 (1981): 491.

23 "The Meaning of Ordination: A Study Paper of the Faith and Order Commission of the World Council of Churches," *Foundation* 12 (April-June 1969): 109.

24 Frank Stagg, "Understanding Call to Ministry," in *Formation for Christian Ministry*, ed. Davis and Rowlett (Louisville, KY: Louisville Southern Baptist Seminary, 1988), 40.

25 "The call to be clergy has more in common with the call of Paul in Acts 9, in which someone is summoned for a specific task

within the church's mission." William H. Willimon, *Pastor: The Theology and Practice of Ordained Ministry*, 16.

26 Cullinan, *Sorting It Out*, 21–22.

27 Roy A. Harrisville, *Ministry in Crisis: Changing Perspectives on Ordination and the Priesthood of All Believers* (Minneapolis, MN: Augsburg Publishing House, 1987), 15.

28 Derek Tidball, in his survey of the New Testament in regard to pastoral leadership, concluded that we do not have enough evidence to claim that overseers and elders are two distinct groups. Derek Tidball, *Ministry by the Book*, 155.

29 Scholars assume that Peter's designation as "fellow elder" is actually an implication of his superiority over the other elders. J. Ramsey Michaels cites New Testament examples where compound *sug*-formations imply a "stratagem of benevolence." See, for example, Revelation 19:10; 22:9, where an angel says that he is a fellow servant with John and his brothers. Thus, Peter is like the bishop of a diocese who stands before the clergy and addresses them as his fellow priests. J. Ramsey Michael, *1 Peter*, Word Biblical Commentary, vol. 49, (Waco, TX: Word Books, 1988), 280.

30 Harrisville, *Ministry in Crisis*, 21–22.

31 Derek Tidball, *Ministry by the Book*, 238.

32 Eugene Peterson and Marva Dawn, *The Unnecessary Pastor: Rediscovering the Call* (Grand Rapids, MI: Eerdmans, 2000), 1–7. See also Howard K. Batson, *Common-Sense Church Growth* (Macon, GA: Smyth & Helwys, 1999), 1–20.

33 Fred B. Craddock, *Craddock Stories* (St. Louis: Chalice Press, 2001), 136–137.

34 As quoted in Winthrop S. Hudson, "The Pastoral Ministry: Call and Ordination," *Foundations* 5 (1962): 242–243.

35 Willimon, "The Spiritual Formation of the Pastor," 35.

36 Willimon, "The Spiritual Formation of the Pastor," 38.

37 Willimon, "The Spiritual Formation of the Pastor," 38.

38 John Ortberg, "Call Forwarding: What It Takes to Call Leaders from Tomorrow's Church Today," *Leadership Journal* 34 (2013): 29.

Chapter 2

[39] Peter G. Northouse, *Leadership: Theory and Practice*, 6th ed. (Thousand Oaks, CA: Sage Publications, 2013), 5.

[40] Jim Collins, *Good to Great and the Social Sectors* (Boulder, CO: Jim Collins, 2005), 13.

[41] Don N. Howell, Jr., *Servants of the Servant: A Biblical Theology of Leadership* (Eugene, OR: Wipf and Stock, 2003), 3. J. Oswald Sanders concurs that the essence of leadership is influence, "Leadership is influence, the ability of one person to influence others." *Spiritual Leadership* (Chicago, IL: Moody, 1967; reprint edition, 1980), 35.

[42] Henry Blackaby and Richard Blackaby, *Spiritual Leadership: Moving People On to God's Agenda* (Nashville, TN: B&H, 2001), 20.

[43] C. Gene Wilkes, *Jesus on Leadership: Timeless Wisdom on Servant Leadership* (Carol Stream, IL: Tyndale, 1998), 20. The starting place for servant leadership as envisioned by Robert K. Greenleaf begins with a "natural desire to serve" rather than a call by God to serve.

[44] Northouse, *Leadership*, 185. The seminal work of James MacGregor Burns, *Leadership* (New York: Harper & Row, 1978), identified the difference between transactional and transformational leadership.

[45] Northouse, *Leadership*, 232–33. Robert K. Greenleaf, in *Servant Leadership: A Journey into the Nature of Legitimate Power and Greatness* (Mahwah, NJ: Paulist Press, 1977), initiated the concept of servant leadership for business, education, and religion.

[46] For example, see Northouse's "Ten Characteristics of a Servant Leader" as identified by L. C. Spears, in Northouse, *Leadership*, 221–222. Also, compare Jesus' life and leadership to what Jim Collins describes as "Level 5 Leadership" in *Good to Great* (New York: HarperBusiness, 2001), 17–40.

[47] James M. Kouzes and Barry Z. Posner, *The Leadership Challenge: How to Get Extraordinary Things Done in Organizations* (San Francisco: Jossey-Bass, 1987), 85.

48 Bill Hybels, *Courageous Leadership* (Grand Rapids, MI: Zondervan, 2002), 32.

49 Ken Blanchard, Bill Hybels, and Phil Hodges, *Leadership by the Book: Tools to Transform Your Workplace* (New York: William Morrow and Co., 1999), 124.

50 Blanchard, Hybels, and Hodges, *Leadership by the Book*, 126.

51 Sanders, *Spiritual Leadership*, 171.

52 Bill George, *Authentic Leadership: Rediscovering the Secrets to Creating Lasting Value* (San Francisco: Jossey-Bass, 2003), 92.

53 Blanchard, Hybels, and Hodges, *Leadership by the Book*, 26.

54 Warren Bennis, *On Becoming a Leader* (Boston, MA: Addison-Wesley Publication Co., 1994), 47.

55 Max DePree, *Leadership Is an Art* (New York: Doubleday, 1989), 10.

56 Ronald A. Heifetz and Marty Linsky, *Leadership on the Line: Staying Alive through the Dangers of Leading* (Boston, MA: Harvard Business School Press, 2002), 20.

57 Sanders, *Spiritual Leadership*, 143.

58 J. Robert Clinton, *The Making of a Leader: Recognizing the Lessons and Stages of Leadership Development* (Colorado Springs, CO: NavPress, 1988), 145.

59 Neal Cole, *Organic Leadership: Leading Naturally Right Where You Are* (Grand Rapids, MI: Baker Books, 2009), Kindle ed., locations 1832–1835.

60 Sanders, *Spiritual Leadership*, 103.

61 Richard Kriegbaum, *Leadership Prayers* (Carol Stream, IL: Tyndale, 1998), 114.

62 Wilkes, *Jesus on Leadership*, 199.

63 Clinton, *The Making of a Leader*, 116.

Chapter 3

64 Douglas L. Fagerstrom, *The Ministry Staff Member* (Grand Rapids, MI: Zondervan, 2006), 48.

65 George Cladis, *Leading the Team-Based Church* (San Francisco: Jossey-Bass, 1999), 97.

66 Jim Collins, *Good to Great* (New York: HarperBusiness, 2001), 41.

67 Harold J. Westing, *Church Staff Handbook: How to Build an Effective Ministry Team* (Grand Rapids, MI: Kregel Publications, 2012), 95.

68 Fagerstrom, *The Ministry Staff Member*, 272.

69 Westing, *Church Staff Handbook*, 96.

70 Wayne Cordeiro, *Doing Church as a Team* (Ventura, CA: Regal, 2004), 20.

71 Fagerstrom, *The Ministry Staff Member*, 302.

72 Peter F. Drucker, *Managing Oneself* (Boston, MA: Harvard Business Review Classics, 2008), 1, 3.

73 Fagerstrom, *The Ministry Staff Member*, 46.

74 Westing, *Church Staff Handbook*, 128.

75 Carl E. Larson and Frank M. J. LaFasto, *When Teams Work Best* (New York: Sage Publications, 2001), 78.

76 Lyle E. Schaller, *The Multiple Staff and the Larger Church* (Nashville, TN: Abingdon Press, 1980), 119–20.

77 Larson and LaFasto, *When Teams Work Best*, 99.

78 Fagerstrom, *The Ministry Staff Member*, 302.

79 Fagerstrom, *The Ministry Staff Member*, 115.

80 Fagerstrom, *The Ministry Staff Member*, 117.

Chapter 4

81 Kevin E. Lawson, *How to Thrive in Associate Staff Ministry* (Herndon, VA: The Alban Institute, 2000), 7.

82 Lawson, *How to Thrive in Associate Staff Ministry*, 217–218.

83 Lawson, *How to Thrive in Associate Staff Ministry*, 23.

84 Lawson, *How to Thrive in Associate Staff Ministry*, 23.

85 Don Cousins, Leith Anderson, and Arthur DeKruyter, *Mastering Church Management* (Portland, OR: Multnomah, 1990), 119.

86 Cousins, Anderson, and DeKruyter, *Mastering Church Management*,119–120.

87 Cousins, Anderson, DeKruyter, *Mastering Church Management*,121-122.

88 J. Ralph Hardee, "Staff Relationships," in Bruce P. Powers, ed. *Church Administration Handbook* (Nashville: Broadman Press, 1985), 274.

89 Wayne Dehoney, "The Pastor as Leader of the Staff," *Review and Expositor* 78, no 1 (1981): 45.

90 Dehoney, "The Pastor as Leader of the Staff," 47.

91 Dehoney, "The Pastor as Leader of the Staff," 46.

92 Dehoney, "The Pastor as Leader of the Staff," 46–47.

93 Hardee, "Staff Relationships," 275.

94 Hardee, "Staff Relationships," 277–282.

95 F. LaFasto and C. Larson, *When Teams Work Best: 6,000 Team Members and Leaders Tell What It Takes to Succeed* (Thousand Oaks, CA: Sage Publications), 2001.

96 William P. Tuck, "A Theology for Healthy Church Staff Relations," *Review and Expositor* 78, no 1 (1981): 5.

97 Tuck, "A Theology for Healthy Church Staff Relations," 7.

98 Tuck, "A Theology for Healthy Church Staff Relations," 8.

99 Tuck, "A Theology for Healthy Church Staff Relations," 8.

100 Tuck, "A Theology for Healthy Church Staff Relations," 8–9.

101 Tuck, "A Theology for Healthy Church Staff Relations," 9.

102 Leonard E. Wedel, *Church Staff Administration: Practical Approaches* (Nashville, TN: Broadman Press, 1978), 147–148.

103 Wedel, *Church Staff Administration*, 149–152.

104 Wedel, *Church Staff Administration*, 154–156.

105 Kenneth K. Killinski and Jerry C. Wofford, *Organization and Leadership in the Local Church* (Grand Rapids, MI: Zondervan, 1973), 178.

106 Wendell L. Boertje, "The Minister of Music in Church Staff Relations: Role and Responsibilities," *Review and Expositor* 78, no 1(1981): 74.

107 Boertje, "The Minister of Music in Church Staff Relations: Role and Responsibilities," 73.

[108] Boertje, "The Minister of Music in Church Staff Relations: Role and Responsibilities," 71.

[109] Joe McKeever, "What can a church staff do to ensure healthy working relationships?" accessed October 1, 2013, http://www.buildingchurchleaders.com/discussion/asktheexperts/joenmckeever/q4.html.

[110] W. L. Howse, *The Church Staff and its Work* (Nashville, TN: Broadman Press, 1959), 149.

[111] Lawson, *How to Thrive in Associate Staff Ministry,* 33.

[112] Mike Bonem and Roger Patterson. *Leading from the Second Chair* (San Francisco, CA: Jossey-Bass, 2005), 22–24.

[113] Bonem and Patterson, *Leading from the Second Chair,* 96–97.

Chapter 5

[114] Jim Collins, *Good to Great: Why Some Companies Make the Leap . . . And Others Don't* (New York: HarperBusiness, 2001), 90-119.

[115] Collins, *Good to Great,* 90-119.

[116] James M. Kouzes and Barry Z. Posner, *The Leadership Challenge: How to Make Extraordinary Things Happen in Organizations,* 5th edition (San Francisco: Jossey-Bass, 2012).

[117] Kouzes and Posner, *The Leadership Challenge.*

[118] Collins, *Good to Great,* 114-116.

Chapter 6

[119] Herschel H. Hobbs, *The Baptist Faith and Message,* 1963 ed. (Nashville, TN: Convention Press, 1971), 64.

[120] "The Church's One Foundation," words by Samuel J. Stone; music by Samuel S. Wesley.

[121] According to *SBCLife,* Journal of the Southern Baptist Convention, the average tenure for a Southern Baptist pastor is just over two years (*SBCLife,* February 2008).

122 "Polity: Form or constitution of the government of a state, or, by extension, of any institution or organization similarly administered; the general or fundamental system or organization of a government as determined by the theory on which it is based as to the object it aims to accomplish, its relation to the people their political and civil rights, etc.; by extension, the constitution or organization in an analogous institution,, esp. in a religious denomination." *Webster's New International Dictionary*, 2nd ed. unabridged (G. & C. Merriam Company, 1934), 1909.

Chapter 7, Part A

123 Webster, *s.v.* "Ethics." Arthur Holmes writes, "Ethics is about the good (that is, what values and virtues we should cultivate) and about the right (that is, what our moral duties may be)." Arthur Holmes, *Ethics: Approaching Moral Decisions*, 2nd ed. (Downers Grove, IL: IVP Academic, 1984), 12.

124 Karen Lebacqz and Joseph D. Driskill, *Ethics and Spiritual Care: A Guide for Pastors, Chaplains, and Spiritual Directors* (Nashville: Abingdon Press, 2000), 37–58.

125 Lebacqz and Driskill, *Ethics and Spiritual Care,* 37–58. The authors point to Urban T. Holmes III, *The Future Shape of Ministry* (New York: Seabury Press, 1971). For contrasting views of a "professional" minister, see John Piper, *Brothers, We are NOT Professionals* (Nashville: Broadman & Holman, 2002), and Joe E. Trull and James E. Carter, *Ministerial Ethics: Moral Formation for Church Leaders,* 2d ed. (Grand Rapids: Baker Academic, 2004), 25–32. Trull and Carter argue that ministers *are* professionals.

126 See Ephesians 4:11–12. Paul wrote that the office of pastor and teacher is a gift to the church to "equip the saints for the work of ministry" (Ephesians 4:12, NRSV).

127 See Walter E. Wiest and Elwyn A. Smith, *Ethics in Ministry* (Minneapolis: Fortress Press, 1990), 126–27.

[128] See *Theological Wordbook of the Old Testament, s.v., mishpat*, by R. Laird Harris, Gleason L. Archer, Jr., and Bruce Waltke (Chicago, IL: Moody Publishers, 2003). The term "authority" (Old Testament, *mishpat*) is frequently associated with right (*sedeq*) and righteousness (*s^{e}daqa*) when describing God's reign and God's dealings with God's creatures. This idea lies at the heart of a true understanding of the biblical worldview. With "rights" come responsibilities in God's created order; therefore, rightness rooted in God's character ought to be an attribute of humankind and of judicial process among them. A biblical understanding of *right* and *rights*, therefore, implies a specific God-initiated relationship with humankind that results in a radical reversal of both worldly *character* and *actions*.

[129] A love (*agape*) and justice (*dike*) model has been postulated as an effective approach to pastor-staff relationships. "Love appeals to altruism in its concerns for other persons; justice is more skeptical about human nature and emphasizes the need to defend other's rights and claims...," according to Wiest and Smith, *Ethics in Ministry*, 127. See William Frankena, *Ethics* (Upper Saddle River, NJ: Prentice Hall, 1973), 56–59. Frankena believes that love is balanced by the principles of beneficence and distributive justice (equality).

[130] Richard M. Gula, *Ethics in Pastoral Ministry* (New York: Paulist Press, 1996), 23.

[131] Gula, *Ethics in Pastoral Ministry*, 24.

[132] Gula, Ethics in Pastoral Ministry, 23–24. See Joseph E. Bush, Jr., *Gentle Shepherding: Pastoral Ethics and Leadership* (St. Louis, MO.: Chalice Press, 2006), 132–134.

[133] Bush, *Gentle Shepherding,* 133.

[134] Gula, *Ethics in Pastoral Ministry,* 75. See Stanley J. Grenz and Roy D. Bell, *Betrayal of Trust: Sexual Misconduct in the Pastorate* (Downers Grove, IL: InterVarsity Press, 1995), 89.

[135] Bush, *Gentle Shepherding,* 115.

[136] Gula, *Ethics in Pastoral Ministry,* 93.

137 Gula, *Ethics in Pastoral Ministry*, 93.

138 Gula, *Ethics in Pastoral Ministry*, 94. Gula cites Peter Rutter, *Sex in the Forbidden Zone* (New York: Ballantine Books, 1997). Ninety-six percent of sexual misconduct cases occur between a man in power and woman under his care.

139 Gula, *Ethics in Pastoral Ministry*, 94. See Joe E. Trull and James E. Carter, *Ministerial Ethics: Moral Formation for Church Leaders* (Grand Rapids, MI: Baker Academic, 2004), 165.

140 Gula, *Ethics in Pastoral Ministry*, 95.

141 I am indebted to the thoughts of Edmund Pellegrino and David Thomasma for this application of Christian justice. See Edmund D. Pellegrino and David C. Thomasma, *Helping and Healing: Religious Commitment in Health Care* (Washington, DC: Georgetown University Press, 1997), 146–50.

Chapter 7, Part B

141 See http://healthychurch.org/threshold/hardest-issue-we-face. Accessed October 7, 2013.

143 One pattern particularly recognized among psychologists is that of toleration, empathy, and support. Toleration may sound too weak, but the quality is higher than hate in tone and application. The other two exhibit value practices that likely have absorbed some Christian guidelines. Another pattern illustrated comes through Guy Greenfield's book *We Need Each Other: Reaching Deeper Levels in Our Interpersonal Relationships* (Grand Rapids, MI: Baker Book House, 1984). Greenfield, a Christian ethicist who practiced his ethics in academic as well as pastoral settings, listed eight levels of relationships: avoidance, greeting, separate interests, common interests, social interactions, caring, sharing, and intimacy. Obviously, these labels cover the many levels of our relationships, all the way from those we avoid or ignore to those with whom we share our deepest thoughts and emotions.

144   Our church culture moves in ignorance regarding a theology of power. This ignorance allows the church and Christians to adapt to cultural modes of power, often more abusive in application than otherwise. This enculturation of "getting things done" has provided as much negative witness to the gospel as perhaps any dynamic issuing from Christians. See William M. Tillman, Jr. "A Theology of Power, Or a Lack Thereof," *Review and Expositor* 108 (2011): 509–518.

145   One example of the contemporary discussion regarding the place of church identifying principles is found in this interview: http://www.religiondispatches.org/archive/atheologies/6933/, accessed October 7, 2013. Although the reader may find a great deal of agreement with this basic discussion, further insight into the larger context can come with this reference: http://www.pewforum.org/Unaffiliated/nones-on-the-rise. aspx#growth, accessed October 7, 2013. The matter of relevancy of contemporary church life is addressed popularly by Terry Mattingly in http://www.patheos.com/blogs/tmatt/2013/03/talking-to-real-live-nones/, accessed October 7, 2013.

146   The term "saints," *hagios*, occurs often in those New Testament texts following the Gospels. After the Gospels come the formation and living out of the *ecclesia*, the church. Too little attention is given to ecclesiology. The term is based in a corporate understanding of the Christian life—a group (or groups) of believers with common purposes in mind. A check of a concordance will show that the word for "saints" occurs often through these narratives.

146   So many of the guidelines from Jesus (for example, *turn the other cheek, walk the second mile*), Paul, and others put into stark contrast the relational values of the surrounding culture. The Hellenistic world was class-based, militaristic, and gender exclusive.

148   Examples of these patterns abound in the Pauline materials. To catch the flavor, tone, and energy from Paul about how congregants should relate to one another and to those outside

the congregation, and much more, read Romans 12–15. Most of the patterns mentioned are found in these chapters.

149 The *koine* Greek equivalents of these terms are *koinonia*, *kerygma*, *didache*, and *diakonia*. Their study will reveal depths to the concepts ordinarily not carried by the English words. The Greek terms are layered in meaning, interfacing to form a holistic concept exhibiting the qualities of Christian character to be useful for the inreach and outreach of any congregation. The character traits listed as a definition of *agape* love in 1 Corinthians 13 contribute to our understandings and implementations of appropriate relationships. Likewise, Galatians 5:22–23, which provides one of the vices and virtues lists, should be enough for us to recognize the standards by which Christians are to treat one another. As we explore the character and its development appropriate for relationships within a congregational context, a guideline that has been used over the centuries is: "In essentials, unity. In nonessentials, liberty. In all things, love." The statement has been attributed to Augustine, though this website notes the lack of connection to Augustine: http://www9.georgetown.edu/faculty/jod/augustine/quote.html, accessed October 7, 2013. Still, whoever originated these thoughts has, with simplicity, neatly encapsulated the guidelines for church relationships.

150 See http://billwilsoncch.wordpress.com/2012/07/30/search-committee-ethics/ for good advice about the ethical work of a search committee. (Accessed October 7, 2013.) The same qualities driving these guidelines of how not to operate as a search committee can inform the group charged with assisting the pastor or other staff to be integrated into the congregation as smoothly as possible. Yet, a congregation need not wait for a search committee to be formed to develop this pastor-church relations group.

151 Barbara Brown Taylor, *The Preaching Life* (Boston, Massachusetts: Cowley Publications, 1993), 77.

152 A microcosmic illustration can serve to highlight the problem of too many forced terminations of ministers. The power abuse

on the part of congregants no doubt has fed into the sensitivities of younger ministers-to-be, who upon learning of the scale of forced terminations leave their intentions, their sense of calling to pastoral ministry. See these statistics: http://www.baptistcourier.com/8049.article, accessed November 19, 2013.

153 Humor is a powerful mechanism for carrying the energy of transcending incongruent ideas, including those that can be polarizing. Forms of humor include riddles, puns, parodies, irony, and paradox. The latter two forms are made to order to be used as part of Christian character building. Sarcasm, an oft-used form, should be avoided. The term finds its base in the Greek word *sarx*, with the added ingredient of meaning "tearing of flesh."

Norman Cousins, in *The Healing Heart: Antidotes to Panic and Helplessness* (New York: W. W. Norton and Company, 2005), reflects on the power of one's belief system to deal with illness. However, most of all, Cousins reminds us of the power of laughter to deal with illness.

I still stand by a comment I made in 1991, based on years of experience before that time: "Humor has not received its proper due among us. It is actually a theological and philosophical category for reflection. Humor assimilates the incongruities of life, the evil and suffering which abound around us, and transcends those with some sense of resolutions. I would maintain, for instance, that the Resurrection is the great punchline of all time. The Destroyer, Death, apparently won. The Apostle Paul maintained, however, 'O, Death, where is thy sting.' A rough paraphrase of that idea is, 'You thought you had us; but you missed!' See William M. Tillman, Jr., "Loss, Grief, and Aids," *Journal of Clergy in Crisis* 2, no. 1 (1991): 11.

Marv Knox has commented helpfully on the matter of church relationships as follows: "Service is an attitude before it's an action. Jesus said people who truly lead and who are valuable in his kingdom are folks who see themselves as last. They're the ones who think first about others and about others' needs. And that's why they serve. They want others to thrive—physically, emotionally, mentally and spiritually. If we were sold out to service, we would start by changing our churches. We'd quit arguing over worship, or the budget, or doctrine, or what people wear on Sunday morning, or whatever your church argues about. If we stood steadfast for service, we'd make sure we know everything about the people in our neighborhood or community. We'd make sure they feel welcome and completely at home in our church house. But even if they never dream of setting foot on our property, we'd do what it takes to make them feel safe, secure, hopeful and loved. And, one day, we would arrive at heaven's gate and hear, 'Well done, good and faithful *servant*.'" Marv Knox, "Service," *Common Call: The Baptist Standard Magazine* (March 2013): 30.

Chapter 8

154 S. Truett Cathy, *Eat More Chicken: Inspire More People* (Decatur, GA: Looking Glass Books, 2002), 36–38.

155 Cathy, *Eat More Chicken*, 194.

156 In addition to the chapter in this book on servant leadership, there are at least two major books on leadership that staff leaders would do well to read. One classic book (1970) by R. K. Greenleaf is *The Servant as Leader*. Another outstanding current (2013) resource is *Leadership Theory and Practice*, by Peter G. Northouse. (See the bibliography for this chapter for information about each of these books.) Both of these books are used in leadership courses across the nation, and both are helping to produce a generation of leaders with integrity and who understand that leaders at best are servants.

157 Alvin G. Lindgren, *Foundations for Purposeful Church Administration* (Nashville, TN: Abingdon Press, 1965), 23.

158 See Leonard Wedel, *Church Staff Administration* (Nashville, TN: Broadman, 1978), 80–81.
159 Wedel, *Church Staff Administration*, 86–87.
160 Cathy, *Eat More Chicken*, 194.

Chapter 9

161 "Selflessness Leads to Spiritual Maturity," *Baptist Press*, http://www.bpnews.net/bpnews.asp?id=39217. Accessed October 11, 2013.
162 Peter Marshall, BrainyQuote.com, Xplore Inc., 2013. Accessed October 11, 2013, http://www.brainyquote.com/quotes/quotes/p/petermarsh158662.html.
163 Michael J. Anthony and James Estep, Jr., ed., *Management Essentials for Christian Ministries* (Nashville, TN: BH Publishing Group, 2005), 44.
164 Robert Welch, *Church Administration: Creating Efficiency for Effective Ministry* (Nashville, TN: BH Publishing Group, 2010), 24.
165 Anthony and Estep, *Management Essentials for Christian Ministries*, 51.
166 Will Mancini, *Church Unique: How Missional Leaders Cast Vision, Capture Culture, and Create Movement* (San Francisco, CA: Jossey-Bass, 2008), 199.
167 Reggie McNeal, *Missional Renaissance: Changing the Scorecard for the Church* (San Francisco, CA: Jossey-Bass, 2009), xvi.
168 McNeal, *Missional Renaissance*, 107.
169 Thom Rainer and Eric Geiger, *Simple Church: Returning to God's Process for Making Disciples* (Nashville, TN: BH Publishing Group, 2011), 255.
170 Audrey Malphurs, *Look Before You Lead: How to Discern & Shape Your Church Culture* (Grand Rapids, MI: Baker Books, 2013), 35.

171 Welch, *Church Administration*, 26.
172 Larry J. Michael, *Spurgeon on Leadership: Key Insights for Christian Leaders from the Prince of Preachers* (Grand Rapids: Kregel, 2003), 101.
173 Holman Christian Standard Bible.
174 George Cladis, *Leading the Team-Based Church: How Pastors and Church Staffs Can Grow Together into a Powerful Fellowship of Leaders* (San Francisco: Jossey-Bass, 1999), 27.
175 Reggie McNeal, *The Present Future: Six Tough Questions for the Church* (San Francisco: Jossey-Bass, 2009).
176 Anthony and Estep, *Management Essentials for Christian Ministries*, 78, quoting Gary Bredfelt.
177 Anthony and Estep, *Management Essentials for Christian Ministries*, 78, quoting Gary Bredfelt.
178 Anthony and Estep, *Management Essentials for Christian Ministries*, 84, quoting Gary Bredfelt.
179 McNeal, *Missional Renaissance*, 102.

Chapter 11

180 James Leo Garrett, Jr., *Baptist Church Discipline*, 2nd ed. (Paris, AR: The Baptist Standard Bearer, Inc., 2004), 5.
181 See Deborah L. Rhode, ed. *Moral Leadership: The Theory and Practice of Power, Judgment, and Policy* (San Francisco: Jossey-Bass, 2006), 4. Leading others is a moral enterprise because relationships are involved, but few leaders have been equipped to *shepherd* their followers through moral heartache (Psalm 23:3).
182 G. Curtis Jones, *The Naked Shepherd: A Pastor Shares His Private Feelings About Living, Working, and Growing Together in the Church* (Waco, TX: Word Books, 1979), 166. Jones quotes Nouwen to illustrate that "the faithful pastor is God's representative, agent of reconciliation, encouragement, and comfort" (166).

183   *Didache*, chapter 2, accessed October 15, 2013, http://www.earlychristianwritings.com/text/didache-roberts.html.

184   Gregory of Nazianzen, *Oration II: In Defence of His Flight to Pontus, and His Return, after His Ordination to the Priesthood, with an Exposition of the Character of the Priestly Office*, vol. 7 of the *Nicene and Post-Nicene Fathers; Cyril of Jerusalem, Gregory Nazianzen*, 2nd series, ed. Philip Schaff and Henry Wace (Peabody, MA: Hendricksen Publishers, Inc., 2004), 207. Gregory (330–390) noted how difficult it was for men to submit to the rule of another, and also how it was more difficult to know how to rule over men. See also Gregory the Great (540–604). See also *The Book of Pastoral Rule of Saint Gregory the Great, Roman Pontiff, to John, Bishop of the City of Ravenna*, vol. 12b of *A Select Library of the Nicene and Post-Nicene Fathers of the Christian Church*, 2d series, *Leo the Great, Gregory the Great*, ed. Schaff and Wace (New York: Christian Literature Company, 1895), 16: "Hence it is needful that when a wound of sin in subordinates is repressed by correction, even constraint should moderate itself with great carefulness, to the end that it may so exercise the rights of discipline against delinquents as to retain the bowels of loving-kindness. For care should be taken that a ruler shew himself to his subjects as a mother in loving-kindness, and as a father in discipline." Both loving discipline and restoration were to be common pastoral duties.

185   Martin Luther, *Works of Martin Luther with Introduction and Notes*, vol. 1 (Philadelphia, PA: A. J. Homan, 1915), 7–9. Luther aimed for "less writing and more studying and reading of the Scriptures."

186   Philip Jacob Spener, *Pia Desideria*, translated, edited, and with an introduction by Theodore G. Tappert (Eugene, OR: Wipf and Stock, Publishers, 1964), 93.

187   Spener, *Pia Desideria*, 83. Spener cites the era of Origen (AD 182–254), where church discipline was very strict. Church members could be excluded from membership until there was sufficient evidence of reform. It is noteworthy that the emphasis was on reform and restoration.

[188] Spener, *Pia Desideria*, 89.

[189] A pastor must set a proper example in both the study and application of the word of God in his own life. Too often, contemporary pastors feel the demands of ministry squeezing out the time for prayer, Bible study, and personal reflection.

[190] William A. Clebsch and Charles R. Jaekle, *Pastoral Care in Historical Perspective* (New York: Harper & Row, Torchbook ed., 1967), 9. The four classic pastoral care functions are healing, guiding, sustaining, and reconciling.

[191] Clebsch and Jaekle, *Pastoral Care in Historical Perspective*, 9.

[192] This attitude is not biblical. Actually, it keeps laypersons from exercising their gifts. On the one hand, the church is often left with vacant positions needing to be filled; and on the other hand, staff members experience burnout trying to cover all the empty openings.

[193] See Gordon MacDonald, *Rebuilding Your Broken World* (Nashville: Oliver Nelson, A Division of Thomas Nelson, 1988), 119. Pastor MacDonald experienced a serious moral fall in his personal ministry and wrote about the dangers of overwork in ministry: "I've spent a large part of my adulthood in a vocation that knows no hourly bounds, no seeming limit to the number of things to do, [and] [*sic*] no point where one can walk away and refuse to see another person." "I've grown increasingly aware that it can exact an enormous toll on spiritual and physical energy reserves."

[194] Hartford Institute for Religion Research, "A Quick Question: How Common is Clergy Sexual Misconduct?" accessed October 14, 2013, http://hirr.hartsem.edu/research/quick_question18.html. Pastors were more often dismissed for abuses of power, making arbitrary decisions about programs and staff, and being unfair supervisors than for sexual misconduct.

[195] Diana R. Garland and Christen Argueta, "How Clergy Sexual Misconduct Happens: A Qualitative Study of First-Hand Accounts," in *Social Work and Christianity*, accessed April 20, 2013, http://www.baylor.edu/content/services/document.php/96038.pdf.

[196] God did not turn a blind eye to the sins of Eli's sons (1 Samuel 2:12–36), to David's adultery with Bathsheba (2 Sam. 11:1–12:23), or to the dishonesty of Ananias and Sapphira (Acts 5:1–11).

[197] Sexual misconduct by a minister requires clearly defined steps to address the sin. See Stanley J. Grenz and Roy D. Bell, *Betrayal of Trust: Sexual Misconduct in the Pastorate* (Downers Grove, IL: InterVarsity Press, 1995). See also Joe E. Trull and James E. Carter, *Ministerial Ethics: Moral Formation for Church Leaders*, 2nd ed. (Grand Rapids, MI: Baker Academic, 2004). Kent R. Hughes and John H. Armstrong, in "Why adulterous pastors should not be restored," *Christianity Today* 39 (April 3, 1995): 33–36, offer the view that a pastor should not be restored to leadership as pastor following sexual misconduct; however, some fallen pastors are called to pastoral leadership in the same church or other churches following a period of discipline and restoration. Understandably, due to the gravity of sexual misconduct, the topic is strongly debated.

[198] See Grenz and Bell, *Betrayal of Trust*, 158. The authors point out that in the Matthew 18 passage, the primary focus is occasions where a believer feels "personally wronged." Clergy sexual misconduct is never merely a private matter, "even though it contains a personal dimension." The biblical text suggests a peer relationship, and this is generally not the case in instances of clergy sexual misconduct. See also Trull and Carter, *Ministerial Ethics*, 181.

[199] Gerhard Kittel, *Theological Dictionary of the New Testament*, trans. and ed. Geoffrey W. Bromiley (Grand Rapids, MI: Wm. B. Eerdmans Publishing Company, 1964), vol. II, *s.v. exousia*

[200] Grenz and Bell, *Betrayal of Trust*, 86.

[201] Grenz and Bell, *Betrayal of Trust*, 87–88.

[202] Grenz and Bell, *Betrayal of Trust*, 87–88. This quote originated from Max Weber's *Economy and Society: An Outline of Interpretive Sociology*, 2 volumes, ed. Guenther Roth and Claus Wittich (Los Angeles: University of California Press, 1978).

[203] Sexual misconduct reflects a classic example of a betrayal of trust. Broken down into its moral components, there is a

distortion of the biblical covenant marriage institution and human sexuality—a betrayal of sexual trust (Genesis 2:18–25).

[204] Grenz and Bell, *Betrayal of Trust*, 103.

[205] Grenz and Bell, *Betrayal of Trust*, 103–104. See also Richard M. Gula, *Ethics in Pastoral Ministry* (New York: Paulist Press, 1996), 22. Gula writes that there are two dimensions about being human: "[W]e are *sacred* and *social*." We are "persons-in-relationship."

[206] Grenz and Bell, *Betrayal of Trust*, 105.

[207] For example, pastors and leaders will want to take the lead in observing organizational policies and biblical principles, even when they appear not to be in their own self-interest.

[208] Trull and Carter, *Ministerial Ethics,* 182. The authors address specifically sexual misconduct, but this approach can be applied to the wider spectrum of moral failure. See also Appendix A, "A Procedure for Responding to Accusations of Clergy Sexual Abuse" (Trull and Carter, *Ministerial Ethics*, 217–220).

[209] Trull and Carter, *Ministerial Ethics,* 182.

[210] Grenz and Bell, *Betrayal of Trust*, 156.

[211] *Editor's note:* Child abuse, including sexual abuse, requires immediate attention and reporting to authorities. See, for example, what is required in Texas, accessed December 2, 2013: https://www.oag.state.tx.us/victims/childabuse.shtml. See also http://texasbaptists.org/clc/keeping-your-church-out-of-court/about/, accessed January 25, 2014, about the publication, *Keeping Your Church Out of Court*, available from the Christian Life Commission of the Baptist General Convention of Texas. Be aware, too, that sexual misconduct by a pastor or staff member in relation to a counseling situation requires reporting to authorities and calls for notifications to future prospective church employers when specific inquiries are made. See http://www.bwwlaw.com/kycooc/news/qna.htm, accessed January 25, 2014.

Made in the USA
Charleston, SC
11 February 2014